Long-ago
Stories of Japan
[Expanded Edition]

Carla Valentine
Coen Nishiumi
Mariko Aoyama

装　　幀＝寄藤文平　垣内　晴
本文イラスト＝菊地玲奈

本書の英文テキストは、ラダーシリーズ『日本昔話1』『日本昔話2』『日本昔話3』から転載しています。
本書は2011年に刊行された、対訳ニッポン『日本昔ばなし』に以下の話を追加し、再編集したものです。

A Tiger on a Paper Screen / The Snow Lady / The Fire Boy / The God of Poverty / Six Little Statues / Twelve Years of Animals / A Gift from Heaven / The Old are Cleverer than the Young / Rice Ball Rolling Down (日本語訳：青山万里子)

日本昔ばなし
【増補改訂版】
Long-ago Stories of Japan
[Expanded Edition]

Carla Valentine
カルラ・ヴァレンタイン＝訳

Coen Nishiumi
西海コエン＝日本語訳

Mariko Aoyama
青山万里子＝日本語訳

まえがき

　世界中どの国や地方にも民話や童話があります。

　人類のルーツを調べる上で、似かよった童話を探して
ゆくことはとても大切なことだといわれています。

　しかし、実は今我々が子供に話して聞かせている童話
は決して太古からあった童話であるとはいえません。
　童話は、歴史の中で子供をどのように教育するべきか
という、その時その時の為政者の影響を強く受け、物語
自体が創作されてきたのです。

　質素や倹約、あるいは謙虚さで人との和を大切にすべ
きという儒教道徳の影響や、因果応報という仏教的な影
響が日本の童話には混在しています。童話は、単に子供
に面白い話をするためにつくられたのではなく、子供を
教育する目的を持って語られてきたのです。ですから、
童話を読めば、その国の文化背景や人々の価値観を読み
とることができるのです。

　また、童話は時には為政者に直裁に利用され脚色され
ます。「桃太郎」のように、大和朝廷が他の部族を平定し

Preface

Every country and region of the world has folklore and fairytales.

It is said that when researching the roots of humankind, it is very important to look for fairytales with similarities in them.

However, it certainly cannot be said that the fairytales we actually tell to our children today are ancient ones. That is because throughout history, the fairytales themselves have been created with strong influences from people in power at that time to show how children should be educated.

The influence of Confucianism's ethic of placing importance on harmonious relations with other people through frugality, thrift, or modesty is mixed with the Buddhist influence of karma, in Japanese fairytales. Fairytales are not just made to be interesting stories for children; they are stories that are told to educate them. For this reason, when you read fairytales, you can understand a country's cultural background and people's values.

Fairytales are often used and modified as propaganda for people in power at that time. It

てゆく過程のなかで、敵を「鬼」と設定した例などはその典型であるといえましょう。そして、「桃太郎」は、明治時代に再び脚色され、日本がアジアに進出するときに、桃太郎を正義の味方である日本人に、鬼を悪い敵になぞらえて語られてゆきました。

　童話にも、こうした歴史の陰があることを知っておくべきかもしれません。

　とはいえ、日本人に様々な影響を与え、我々にとっても懐かしい童話の数々を英語で語ることは素敵な試みです。アメリカのように、様々な国からの人が集まって生活しているところでは、それぞれの人のルーツや文化を語りあうために、教育の場でよく出身国の童話などが紹介されます。

　海外に行き、交流するときに、向こうの子供に英語で日本の童話を語ってあげることは、相手の人からも喜ばれるに違いありません。

　ぜひ、本書で、昔の記憶を呼びおこし、思いだした童話をさらに英語で語る練習をしてみてはいかがでしょうか。

IBCパブリッシング編集部

can be said that the process by which the Yamato Court subjugated clans in each area and made the enemies into "ogres" in stories like "Momotaro" is a typical example of this type of thing. "Momotaro" was also dramatized again in the Meiji period, and when Japan invaded Asia, the story was told with Momotaro being linked to Japanese people as a hero of justice, and the ogres to evil enemies.

It is probably a good idea to keep in mind that this kind of history is hidden in fairytales as well.

Anyway, these stories have influenced Japanese people in many ways, and it can be fantastic to try telling the stories that make us feel so nostalgic in English. Like in America, where there are people from various countries living together, in order to talk together about the roots and cultures of various peoples, fairytales from people's countries of origin are often introduced in educational settings.

When you go abroad and interact with foreigners, telling the children Japanese fairytales in English will definitely make the listeners happy too.

By all means, please wake up your memories of the past with this book and also practice trying to tell the fairytales you have remembered in English.

IBC Publishing

目次

Contents

Momotaro

桃太郎

桃太郎

　昔々、あるところに、おじいさんとおばあさん
が住んでおりました。二人の家は、山と川とには
さまれたところにありました。毎日、おじいさん
は山に薪をとりに、おばあさんは川に洗濯に行っ
ておりました。

　ある日のこと、いつものようにおばあさんは川
へとおりていきました。そして、洗濯をおえて顔
をあげると、大きな桃が見えるではありませんか。
桃は水の中で、浮いたり回ったり。重そうで丸く
て桃いろ。とてもおいしそうです。でも、おばあ
さんは桃に手が届きません。

　「おいで。おいで。こっちじゃよ」おばあさんは
呼んでいます。「こっちの水は甘いよ！」
　するとなんと大きな桃は、おばあさんの方に動
きはじめるではありませんか。それは、浮いたり
回ったり。回ったり浮いたり。そしておばあさん
の腕のところにまっすぐやってきたのです。おば

Long, long ago somewhere, there lived an old man and woman. The old couple's house stood between a mountain and a river. Each day, the old man went up the mountain to cut wood, and the old woman went down to the river to wash clothes.

One day, as always, the old woman was down at the river. When she finished the wash, she looked up and saw a great big peach. The peach was bobbing and rolling in the water. It was heavy and round and pink, and it looked delicious. But it was just out of reach.

"Come over here!" the old woman called out. "The water's sweeter over here!"

And, sure enough, the great peach began to move toward her. It bobbed and rolled and rolled and bobbed, straight into her arms. The old woman pulled the peach out of the

あさんは、桃を水から引きあげて、にっこり。早くこのすてきな桃をおじいさんと食べたいなと思いました。

　日も暮れたころ、おじいさんは薪を背おって家にもどってきました。おばあさんが桃を見せるとおじいさんはびっくり。桃を両手で持ちあげて言いました。

water and smiled. She couldn't wait to share this wonderful fruit with her husband.

That evening, as always, the old man came home with a load of wood on his back. When his wife showed him the peach, he couldn't believe his eyes. He picked it up and held it in both hands.

「なんて大きな桃じゃろう。新しいうちに食べてしまおう」

おじいさんは桃を食卓において包丁を持ってきました。すると、桃が動きはじめるではありませんか。

「なんじゃ。なんじゃ」おばあさんが言いました。

「これは生きておるぞ」おじいさんは叫びました。

すると、桃がいきなり二つに裂けて、元気な男の赤ちゃんが飛びだしてきたのです。

「わーーーん」赤ちゃんは太鼓のような大きな声で泣いています。

おじいさんとおばあさんは、もちろんびっくり仰天。でも、とってもうれしい！

「いつもいつも、子どもを授けてくださいとお祈りしていたからねえ」おばあさんはそう言いました。

「神さまがくだされたのじゃ。さあ産湯がいるぞ」

おじいさんがそう言って、火をおこしてお湯を沸かしました。お湯をたらいにいれて、おばあさんが赤ちゃんをお湯にいれようとしたとき、赤ちゃ

"Look at the size of it!" he said. "Let's eat it while it's fresh!"

He placed the peach on the table and picked up a knife. But just then the peach began to move.

"What's happening?" said the old woman.

"It's alive!" her husband shouted.

Suddenly the peach broke in two, and a healthy baby boy jumped out!

"WAAAAAH!" cried the baby, with a voice as loud as a drum.

The old man and woman were, of course, very surprised. But they were also very happy.

"We always prayed for a child of our own!" the old woman said.

"He's a gift from the gods!" said her husband. "Let's prepare his first bath!"

The old man made a fire and heated some water. When he filled the tub, his wife reached for the baby. But the baby pushed her

んはそれをはねのけて、自分でお湯のなかに入っ
てゆきました。

　「まあ、なんて力のある子なのじゃ」おじいさん
とおばあさんは見つめあって大笑い。

　「なんて名前にしましょうか」おばあさんがそう
言うと、

　「そうじゃな。桃から生まれたから、桃太郎とし
よう」とおじいさんは答えます。

＊

　おじいさんとおばあさんは桃太郎をとても大切
に育て、桃太郎は元気な強い子に育ちました。小
さい頃から、桃太郎は村いちばんの相撲とり。12
歳になったときには、国じゅうの男たちの誰も、
桃太郎を投げたおすことができなくなりました。
それで、国じゅうの誰よりも桃太郎はやさしくて
親切。

　14歳になったときのことでした。桃太郎はおじ
いさんとおばあさんの前に座って、深くおじぎを
します。

　「おばあさん。そしておじいさん。しばらくお暇
をいただきたいのです」桃太郎はそう言います。

away and climbed into the hot water all by himself.

"Such power!" the old couple laughed and looked at each other.

"What shall we name him?" the old woman said.

"Well, he was born from a peach," said the old man. "So let's call him Momotaro."

*

Thanks to the old couple's loving care, the "Peach Boy" grew up healthy and strong. Even when he was little, Momotaro was the best sumo wrestler in the village. By the time he was twelve, no man in all of Japan could throw him. And yet he was the sweetest, kindest boy in the land.

Momotaro was only fourteen when he went before the old man and woman and bowed deeply.

"Grandmother, Grandfather," he said. "I must leave you for a while."

「なんじゃと。どこに行こうというのじゃ」おばあさんはたずねます。

「鬼ヶ島に」

「鬼ヶ島とや。何のために」おじいさんはびっくりして叫びました。

「鬼退治。そして宝物を持って帰ります」桃太郎はそう言いました。

その頃、鬼は人々のところにやってきては、金銀、そして宝石を無理矢理奪っていたのです。人々は皆、鬼のことをたいそう怖がっていました。

「鬼ヶ島は遠いぞ」おじいさんは言いました。

「それに、そんな危ないことを」おばあさんも言いました。

「ご心配なく」桃太郎は言いました。「すぐに宝を持ってもどってまいりますから」

おじいさんもおばあさんも、桃太郎が、鬼ヶ島に行くことはいやでした。しかし、桃太郎を止めることはできないと思いました。桃太郎は決して夢をあきらめないからです。そこで、おじいさんは桃太郎に剣とひとそろいの鎧をわたしました。

"What?" said the old woman. "But where will you go?"

"To Demons Island."

"Demons Island?" cried the old man. "Whatever for?"

"To fight the demons," said Momotaro, "and bring back all the treasure."

In those days, you see, demons often came to people. They pushed the people around and took away their gold and silver and jewels. Everyone was afraid of them.

"But Demons Island is so far!" said the old man.

"And so dangerous!" said the old woman.

"Please don't worry," said Momotaro. "I'll be home with the treasure in no time."

The old man and woman didn't want their boy to go, but they knew they couldn't stop him. Momotaro always followed his dreams. So the old man gave him a sword and a suit of armor, and the old woman made him some

　そしておばあさんは、きびだんごをつくってくれ
ました。きびだんごは、桃太郎の大好物だったの
です。それにおばあさんは、桃太郎のために旗も
つくってくれました。その旗には桃の絵と日本一
という文字が描かれています。
　「日本一の桃太郎」です。
＊
　桃太郎は、きびだんごをいれた包みを腰に巻い
て、旗を高々と掲げ、旅にでます。やがて村から
山に入ってゆきます。

　山道をのぼってゆくと、犬が突然薮から出てき
ます。
　「ワン！　ワン！　桃太郎、どこに行くの」

　「鬼ヶ島に鬼退治」
　「すごいね。包みに入っているものは？」
　「日本一のきびだんご」
　「一つおくれよ。ワン！　そしたら僕もついてく
よ」
　「ほら、お食べ。そして僕についといで」
＊

millet dumplings—his favorite food. She also
made a flag for Momotaro to carry. On the
flag was a picture of a peach and the words
Nippon Ichi.

That means "Number One in Japan."

*

The Peach Boy tied the bag of millet dumplings to his belt, held the flag high, and set
out on his journey. He soon left the village
behind and started up the mountain.

Now he was climbing the mountain pass.
Suddenly a dog came out of the brush.

"*Arf! Arf!* Where are you going, Momotaro?"

"To Demons Island, to fight the demons."

"Interesting! What's in the bag?"

"The best millet dumplings in all Japan."

"Give me one—*Arf!*—and I'll go with
you!"

"Here you are, friend. Now follow me!"

*

　それから桃太郎と犬は森のなかを歩いてゆきます。すると突然お猿さんが木からおりてきます。

　「キー！　キー！　桃太郎、どこに行くの」

　「鬼ヶ島に鬼退治」
　「すごいね。包みに入っているものは？」
　「日本一のきびだんご」
　「一つおくれよ。キー！　そしたら僕もついてくよ」

　「ほら、お食べ。そして僕についといで」

＊

　桃太郎と犬とお猿さんは広い野原を歩きます。すると突然雉（キジ）が空から飛んできます。

　「ギー！　ギー！　桃太郎、どこに行くの」

　「鬼ヶ島に鬼退治」
　「すごいね。包みに入っているものは？」
　「日本一のきびだんご」
　「一つおくれよ。ギー！　そしたら僕もついてくよ」

Now Momotaro and the dog were marching through a forest. Suddenly a monkey climbed down from a tree.

"*Key! Key!* Where are you going, Momotaro?"

"To Demons Island, to fight the demons."

"Interesting! What's in the bag?"

"The best millet dumplings in all Japan."

"Give me one—*Key!*—and I'll go with you!"

"Here you are, friend. Now follow me!"

*

Now Momotaro and the dog and monkey were marching across a wide green plain. Suddenly a pheasant flew down from the sky.

"*Whirr! Whirr!* Where are you going, Momotaro?"

"To Demons Island, to fight the demons."

"Interesting! What's in the bag?"

"The best millet dumplings in all Japan."

"Give me one—*Whirr!*—and I'll go with you."

「ほら、お食べ。そして僕についといで」

桃太郎と犬とお猿さん、そして雉は一緒に海辺へ歩いてゆきます。そこには立派な船がありました。

「よし、みんな、船に乗ろう！」桃太郎は号令します。「鬼ヶ島目ざして、出航だ！」

天気はよく、風もあり、船は矢のように速く青い海をわたってゆきます。犬は櫓をこぎ、お猿さんは舵をとり、そして雉は見はりをします。やがて雉が叫びます。

「ギー！ ギー！ 島が見えたぞ」

桃太郎は舳先に走って、鬼がつくった城の高く黒い城壁を見つけます。

「あれだ。真正面があの鬼ヶ島だ！」

犬はオールを漕いで、ワン！ ワン！ お猿さんは船をまっすぐ進めてキー！ キー！ そして雉は島を目指して飛びだします。

"Here you are, friend. Now follow me!"

Now Momotaro and the dog and monkey and pheasant were marching down to the sea. A fine ship was waiting there on the beach.

"All aboard!" said Momotaro. "We'll sail the ship to Demons Island!"

It was a fine day, with a good wind. The ship raced like an arrow across the deep blue sea. The dog was rowing, the monkey was steering, and the pheasant was standing watch. Before very long, the pheasant called out:

"*Whirr! Whirr!* I see an island!"

Momotaro ran to the bow. He could just make out the high black walls of Demons Castle.

"That's it!" he shouted. "Demons Island dead ahead!"

The dog pulled on the oar—*Arf! Arf!* The monkey held the ship steady—*Key! Key!* And the pheasant flew ahead to the island.

　浜にいた鬼は雉を見つけることはできません。でも、船を見たのでびっくりして急ぎお城に逃げて、黒い門の鍵をかけます。船が、鬼ヶ島につくと、桃太郎と犬とお猿さんは船から飛びおり、お城に向かって進軍します。

　「門を開けるんだ！」犬はそう叫んで門をけります。「門を開けるか、さもなければ戦<ruby>いくさ</ruby>になるぞ」

　鬼は門を内側から押さえて開けません。すると雉がお城の塔から飛びおりてきて、鬼たちの目をつつきます。

　「痛い！　逃げるんだ」鬼は叫びます。

　さあ、お猿さんの出番です。お猿さんは壁をのぼって門を内側から開きます。

　「桃太郎。ここに見参！」犬はそう言うと、桃太郎はお城の中に入ってゆきます。

＊

The demons on the beach didn't see the pheasant. But they saw the ship, and they were very afraid. They ran inside their castle and locked the big black gate. When the ship landed, Momotaro and the dog and monkey jumped out. They marched right up to the castle.

"Open up!" the dog shouted and kicked at the gate. "Open up, or prepare for war!"

The demons pushed against the gate from inside, to hold it closed. But the pheasant flew down from the castle tower and pecked at their eyes.

"It hurts!" the demons cried. "Run for your lives!"

Now it was the monkey's turn. He climbed over the wall and opened the gate from inside.

"Momotaro of Japan!" the dog called out as the Peach Boy marched into the grounds.

*

　鬼の王さまが桃太郎たちに会いに出てきます。10人、あるいは12人の強そうな鬼を従えて。鬼は皆金棒を持っています。

「お前は何ものだ」鬼の王さまが口を開きます。

「僕は日本一の桃太郎。宝を返してもらいにやってきた」

「返してもらいたければ、戦ってからだ」鬼の王さまは金棒を振りあげます。

「お望みなら」桃太郎はそう言うと、戦いがはじまりました。

　鬼たちは大きくて意地悪です。しかし、皆心は強くありません。雉が飛んできては、ギー！ギー！といって鬼たちの目をつつきます。犬は走ってくると、ワン！ワン！といって、鬼たちの足に噛みつきます。そしてお猿さんは飛びかかりながら、キー！キー！といって、鬼の顔を引っかきます。

　すると鬼は金棒を投げだして泣きながら逃げてゆきます。

　鬼の王さまだけが取りのこされました。王さま

The King of Demons stepped out of the castle to meet them. He had ten or twelve of his biggest, strongest demons with him. All of them carried iron clubs.

"Who do you think you are?" said the king.

"I'm Momotaro of Japan. And I've come to take back our treasure."

"Not without a fight, you won't!" The king held up his club.

"As you wish," said Momotaro, and the fight began.

Demons are big and mean, but they're weak of heart. The pheasant flew from one to another—*Whirr! Whirr!*—and pecked at their eyes. The dog ran from one to another—*Arf! Arf!*—and bit their legs. And the monkey jumped from one to another—*Key! Key!*—and scratched their faces.

Before very long, the demons all threw down their clubs and ran away in tears.

The only one left was the king himself. He

は前にでて、金棒で桃太郎をたたこうとします。すると桃太郎は飛びのくと、そのまま王さまを地面に投げとばします。そして、王さまの頭を強い腕で押さえつけます。

　「やめてくれ！　降参だ！」鬼の王さまは叫びます。「お前の勝ちだ。桃太郎。命だけは助けてくれ。宝は返すから」

stepped forward and tried to hit Momotaro with his club. But Momotaro jumped out of the way and threw him to the ground. Then he locked the king's head in his powerful arm.

"Stop! I give up!" cried the king. "You win, Momotaro! Please don't kill me! You can have the treasure!"

　桃太郎はついに手をゆるめます。王さまは手を
ついて桃太郎に何度も感謝します。そして家来の
鬼たちに、お城にある金銀財宝を荷車に積むよう
に命令します。鬼たちはその荷車を船に積みこみ
ます。

　「二度とあなたの国の人々を苦しませません」そ
う鬼の王さまは誓ったのです。

　「きっとだぞ」そう言うと、桃太郎は犬とお猿さ
んと雉といっしょに船に飛びのり、帰ってゆきま
す。

*

　故郷では、おじいさんとおばあさんが桃太郎の
帰りを待っていました。

　「無事だといいのだが。いったいいつ帰ってくる
のやら」おばあさんがそう言うと、

　「おや！　帰ってきたぞ」とおじいさんが答えま
す。

　桃太郎は丘から村へと行進してきていたのです。
桃太郎のうしろには、金銀財宝がうず高く積まれ
た荷車を犬とお猿さんが引っぱっています。その
うえの青い空を雉が輪を描いて飛んでいます。

Finally Momotaro let go. The king got down on all fours and thanked him again and again. Then he ordered his demons to fill a cart with all the gold and silver and jewels in the castle. They loaded the cart on the ship.

"We'll never bother your people again!" the King of Demons promised.

"See that you don't," said Momotaro. And he and the dog and monkey and pheasant jumped on the ship and sailed for home.

*

Back home, the old man and woman were waiting for their Peach Boy.

"I hope he's all right," the old woman said. "Oh, when will he return?"

"Look!" said the old man. "Here he comes now!"

Momotaro was marching down the hill toward the village. Behind him, the dog and monkey were pulling a cart full of gold and silver and jewels. Above the cart, in the clear blue sky, the pheasant flew in circles.

　「おお我が子よ」おじいさんは叫びます。「お前ならやれると思っていたよ。桃太郎！」

　「無事でなによりじゃ」おばあさんもそう言います。

　皆大喜び、桜の花も満開でした。

"That's our boy!" cried the old man. "We knew you could do it, Momotaro!"

"We're so glad you're safe!" the old woman said.

Everyone cheered, and the cherry trees were blooming.

A Sparrow with Her Tongue Cut Out

舌きり雀

　昔々、ある村に、やさしいおじいさんと、いじわるなおばあさんが住んでいました。おじいさんは、雀が好きで、子どものようにかわいがっていました。でも、おばあさんは雀が大嫌いです。

　ある日のこと、雀が庭におりてきて、おばあさんが洗濯に使おうとしていた糊（のり）を食べてしまいました。おばあさんは、とても腹がたって、雀をつかまえると舌を切って、追いはらいました。雀は山に飛んでゆきます。

　やさしいおじいさんは、その話を聞いて、雀がとても可哀想になりました。そこで雀を見つけて、おばあさんのやったことを謝ろうと思いました。
　おじいさんは森に行って、人に、舌を切られた雀のお宿はとたずねます。そして、苦労してやっと雀のお宿を見つけました。

　「ここにお詫びにきたのだよ。大丈夫かい？　ど

Long, long ago, there lived a kind old man and his mean old wife in a village. The old man loved sparrows and took care of them like his own children, but his wife hated them.

One day a sparrow flew to their garden and ate the starch while she was washing clothes. She got so angry that she caught the sparrow and cut her tongue out. Then she let it go. The sparrow flew toward the mountains.

The kind old man heard the story and felt very sorry for the sparrow. He decided to find her and say sorry to her for it.

As he was walking in the forest, he asked people, "Where is the house of the sparrow with its tongue cut out?" It was difficult, but he finally found the sparrow's house.

"I came here to say sorry to you. Are you

うか許しておくれ」おじいさんは、そう言いました。

　「来てくれてありがとう。とても驚いたけど、あれは私が悪かったんです。どうか、ここで夕ご飯を食べていってください」雀がそう言うので、おじいさんは、雀のお宿に一晩泊まることにしました。

　次の日の朝、おじいさんが家に帰ろうとすると、雀が言います。「おじいさん、お土産がありますよ。大きいつづらと小さいつづら、どちらがお好き」

　「お土産なんて。でも、どうしてもと言うなら、小さい方をくださいな」

　おじいさんは、つづらを背おって帰りました。そしてなかを見ると、たくさんのお金や金や銀、そして織物などが入っているではありませんか。

　それを見たおばあさんがおじいさんに言いました。「どうして大きなつづらをもらわなかったのかい。これから行ってとってこよう」

　おばあさんは森へ行くと、人に「舌を切られた雀のお宿はどこかいな」とたずねます。そして雀に会いました。

all right? Please forgive us," he said.

"Thank you for coming here. I was shocked, but it was my fault. Why don't you eat some of our dinner?" said the sparrow. The old man stayed there that night.

Before he returned to his house next morning, the sparrow said to him, "These are presents for you. Which do you want, the big box or the small box?"

"I don't want either of them. But if I have to take one, I want the small one," said the man.

He came home with a box on his back. He opened it to find a lot of money, gold, silver, clothes and so on in it.

The old woman asked him, "Why didn't you take the big one? I will go and get it."

As she was walking in the forest, she asked people, "Where is the house of the sparrow with her tongue cut out?" She met the sparrow.

「何しに来たの」雀はたずねます。

「私はお前に会いたかったんだよ。あんなにいろいろと面倒をみたんだから」とおばあさんは言いました。

「それならお入りなさい」雀はそう言います。

するとおばあさんは、「わしもお土産がほしいのじゃ。大きなつづらがの」

おばあさんは、大きくて重いつづらを背中に背おって、雀の宿をあとにします。

家に帰る途中、おばあさんは一刻もはやくつづらの中が見たくて仕方がありません。そこで、道の上につづらをおろすと、それを開けてみたのです。驚いたことに、蛇やお化け、そしてムカデなどなど、怖いものが次から次へと出てくるではありませんか。おばあさんは気を失ってしまったということです。

"Why did you come here?" asked the sparrow.

"I wanted to see you because I took such good care of you," answered the old woman.

The sparrow said, "OK. Come in, please."

The old woman said, "I want a present, too. I want a big box."

She left the sparrow's house carrying the big, heavy box on her back.

On her way home, she couldn't help looking inside the box. She put it down on the road and opened it. To her surprise, snakes, ghosts, centipedes, other terrible things came out of the box one after another. She fainted.

Monkey vs. Crab

猿蟹合戦

　昔々、ある村に蟹が住んでいました。ある日、蟹は、道におにぎりが落ちているのを見つけました。家に帰っていると、猿が声をかけてくるではありませんか。猿は、柿の種をもっていて、おにぎりがほしいので、蟹にそれをおくれと頼みました。そして蟹はお返しに柿の種をもらったのです。

　やがて、蟹は柿の種を庭に植えて、何年も毎日水をやりました。それは大きな木になって、たくさんの柿の実をつけたのです。

　そこに猿がやってきて、木にのぼって、柿をすべて食べてしまいました。そして、ひどいことに、柿の実を力いっぱい蟹に向かって投げつけたので、蟹は死んでしまいました。

　蟹が殺されたことを知った蟹の子どもたちはとても怒ります。そこで友だちの臼と蜂、そして栗に加勢を頼みます。猿が外に出ているあいだ、皆は猿の家に隠れて、猿が帰ってくるのを待ちました。

Long, long ago, there was a crab living in a village. One day she found a rice ball on the road. On her way home she heard a monkey call her name. He had found a persimmon seed. He wanted to eat the rice ball, so he told her that she had to give him the rice ball. She did, and he gave her the seed.

Later, she planted it in her garden and gave it water every day for several years. It became a big tree with a lot of fruit.

The monkey came and climbed the tree. He ate up all the fruit. He was so mean that he threw the fruit at her as hard as he could and killed her.

Now her young crabs were very angry because the monkey had killed her. They asked their friends, a mortar, a bee, and a chestnut to help them. While he was out, they hid in each part of the monkey's house

　やがて、猿は家にもどってきました。そしているりの前に座って体を温めようとします。そこに焼けた栗が飛びだして、猿のお尻を焼いてしまいます。

　猿は痛いよと叫びながら、薬箱に飛んでいって、それを開けました。しかし、そこで蜂が出てきて、猿の肩のところを針で刺します。

　猿は痛いよと叫びながら、水の入ったバケツまで走ってゆきました。しかし、そこで子どもの蟹が出てきて猿の体をのぼると、ハサミで毛や皮や耳を切りおとしてしまいます。

　猿はまた痛いよと叫ぶと、戸へと走って、家から飛びだします。そこに、屋根から大きな臼が飛びおりて、猿を殺してしまいましたとさ。

and waited for him to come home.

Soon the monkey returned and sat in front of the cooking fire to warm himself. The hot chestnut jumped out and burned his bum.

The monkey shouted with pain and ran to a medicine box and opened it, but the bee came out and stung him in the shoulder.

The monkey shouted with pain again and ran to the water bucket, but the young crabs came out from under it and climbed up his body. They pulled his hair, skin and ears with their hands.

The monkey shouted in pain one more time and rushed out of the door of the house. The big mortar jumped off the roof and killed him.

The Crane
Gives Back

鶴の恩返し

　昔々のこと、貧しい若者が山間の小さな家に住んでいました。両親とは死に別れ、一人寂しく暮らしていました。毎日若者は森へ行って木をあつめ、それを近くの町で売ってはなんとか生活をしていました。

　それは冬の初めの朝のこと。若者は雪ふる森を歩いていると、変な物音がするではありませんか。それは誰かが痛がっているような声です。音のする方に歩いてゆくと、そこにはきれいな白い鶴が雪の上に横たわっています。そして羽には矢が刺さっていたのです。

　「ああ、かわいそうに。誰がこんなことを」若者はそう言うと、鶴を腕に抱きかかえ、ゆっくりと矢を抜いてやりました。そして羽の傷を洗って、雪の中にもどしてやると、ゆっくりと鶴のもとを離れます。すると、鶴は羽を広げて、飛びたちます。

Once upon a time, a poor young man lived in a little house in the mountains. His parents were both dead now, and the young man was very lonely. Each day he walked through the forest and collected wood. He sold the wood in the nearest town, and made just enough money to get by.

It was a morning in early winter. The young man was walking through the snowy woods, when he heard something strange. It sounded like a cry of pain. He followed the sound until he discovered a beautiful white crane. She was lying in the snow, with an arrow through her wing.

"You poor thing!" the young man said. "Who did this to you?"

He held the crane in his arms and gently pulled the arrow out. Then he cleaned her wing, set her down in the snow, and stepped

そして、鶴は若者のうえで輪を描き、鳴くと、そのまま雲のなかに消えていきました。

　夜遅く、若者は家で火のそばに座っていました。天気はとても悪く、空には白い雪が舞い、強い風も吹いています。

*

　と、誰かが戸を叩いています。若者は戸を開けてびっくり。とても美しい女の人がそこに立っているではありませんか。

back. The crane spread her wings and rose up into the air. She circled above the young man once, cried out, and flew off into the clouds.

Late that night, the young man was sitting by his fire at home. Outside, the weather was very bad. The sky was white with snow, and a strong wind was blowing.

*

Suddenly there was a knock at the door. When the young man opened it, he was very surprised. A beautiful young woman was standing on the front step.

「道に迷ってしまいました。一晩泊めていただけませんでしょうか」

「どうぞどうぞ」若者はそう言うと女の人を招きいれ、火の側に座らせて、あったかいお汁を持ってきました。

「ありがとうございます。本当にご親切に」女の人はお礼を言います。

「どうか気になさらずに、好きなだけここにいてください」若者はそう応えます。

実は、その後も天気はなかなかよくならず、女の人は何日もそこに滞在したのです。女の人は掃除や料理を手つだいます。若者にとって、その女の人と一緒にいるのは、とても楽しいことです。いなくなったらどんなに寂しいだろうと何度も思います。しかし、ある朝女の人がやってきて、「私を嫁にしてください」と言ったのです。

若者は顔を真っ赤にして、

「私は貧しく、あなたを幸せにはできません」と言いました。

「貧しさなんてどうでもいいんです。一緒にいられれば」

"I have lost my way," she said. "May I spend the night here?"

"Of course!" said the young man. He invited her in, gave her a seat by the fire, and served her some hot soup.

"Thank you so much," she said. "You're very kind."

"You're most welcome," he told her. "Please stay as long as you like."

In fact the bad weather continued, and the woman stayed for many days. She helped with the cleaning and cooking, and she was very good company for the young man. He often thought how sad he would be when she left. But then, one morning, she came to him and said:

"Please take me as your wife."

The young man's face turned bright red.

"I'm a poor man," he said. "I can't give you a good life."

"I don't care if we're poor," she told him, "as long as we can be together."

　そして二人は一緒になりました。

＊

　二人はとても幸せな夫婦でした。しかし、それはとても長く寒い冬でした。しかも正月がやってこようというのに、お金も食べ物もほとんどありません。ある日、若者は心配のあまり妻に言いました。

「食べていけないかもしれないな」

　妻はしばらくの間考えたあと、

「たしか奥の部屋に、はた織り機がありましたね」と言いました。

「あるよ。あれは母親のものだった」若者はそう応えます。

「私にそれで布を織らせてください」と妻は言います。「でも一つだけ約束してほしいのです。私が織物をしているとき、決してなかを見ないでください。絶対に。お願いです」

　若者は不思議に思いましたが、約束します。妻は小部屋に移って戸を閉めます。そしてそれから三日間出てきません。その間、若者は妻の姿をまったく見ることはなく、しかしはた織りの音は昼

And so they married.

*

They were very happy as man and wife. But it was a long, cold winter. Now New Year's was coming, and they had no money and very little food. One day, the young man told his wife that he was worried.

"How will we eat?" he said.

His wife thought for a while before speaking.

"There is an old loom in the little room in back," she said.

"Yes," he said. "It was my mother's."

"I want to use it to weave some cloth," she told him. "But you must promise me one thing. Never look into that room when I'm weaving. This is very important. Please promise."

The young man thought this strange, but he gave her his word. His wife went into the little room and closed the door. And there she stayed for the next three days. The young

に夜に響いてきます。

　三日目の夜、妻はやっと部屋から出てきました。とても弱々しく疲れています。しかし妻はにこっと笑って、三反<ruby>反<rt>たん</rt></ruby>の白い布地を若者に手わたしました。
「これを町で売ってください」

　とても美しい布地でした。月明かりのようにきめ細かく、そしてやわらかく。その翌日、若者は反物を町のお金持ちの家に持ってゆきました。そしてその夜、大きな袋を三つ、どれもお米をいっぱいつめて帰ってきたのです。

「大切な妻よ、本当にありがとう。これで今年の冬もこせよう。そしてお金持ちがもっとこの反物をほしがっている。できるだけ早くまた織っておくれ。とてもよいお金になるから」

　それを聞いた妻は、しばらく無言で、そのあと悲しそうに笑みを浮かべます。
「お望みなら、今すぐに」と言って、奥にある小

man didn't see her in all that time, but he heard the sound of the loom day and night.

On the third night, his wife finally stepped out of the room. She looked weak and tired. But she smiled as she handed him three rolls of white cloth.

"Please take this to town and sell it," she said.

It was very beautiful cloth—as fine and soft as the light of the moon. The next day, her husband carried the rolls straight to the house of the town's richest man. And that night he came home with three big bags full of rice.

"My dear wife!" he said. "Thanks to you, we'll get through the winter. And the rich man wants to buy more! Please weave more cloth as soon as you can! Think of the money we can get for it!"

His wife said nothing at first. But then she smiled sadly.

"Of course. I'll begin right away," she said

さな部屋の戸へと歩いてゆきます。「でも、忘れな
いで。反物を織っているあいだ、決してなかを見
ないと……」

*

　一晩中、そしてその翌日も、若者ははた織りの
音を聞きました。しかし、今度の音は前とは違い
ます。ゆっくりと、重々しく。若者は妻のことが
気になりました。そして、夜遅く、若者は痛みに
泣く声を聞いたのです。約束を守るべきか、それ
ともと思いながら、若者は部屋を見ずにはいられ
ませんでした。

　そして、部屋の戸を開けたとき、若者はびっくり。
妻はそこにはいませんでした。はた織り機のまえ
に座っていたのは、白い鶴だったのです。鶴は病
気になったように弱々しく、その体からは多くの
羽がなくなっていました。鶴は若者を見あげると、
悲しそうに鳴きました。そして若者の目のまえで
あの美しい妻にもどったのです。

　若者は言葉も出ません。
「お前は……お前は」

and walked to the door of the little room in back. "But please remember. You must never look in when I'm weaving..."

*

All that night and all the next day, the young man heard the sound of the loom. But the sound was different this time. It was slower, and heavier. He began to worry about his wife. And then, late in the evening, he heard another sound, like a cry of pain. Promise or no promise, he had to look into the room.

But what a shock he got when he opened the door! His wife wasn't there, but a white crane was sitting at the loom. The crane looked ill and weak, and many of her feathers were gone. When she looked up and saw the young man, she let out a sad cry. And then, right before his eyes, she turned back into his beautiful wife.

The young man couldn't even speak.

"You..." he said. "You're..."

　「そう」妻は言いました。「私は鶴です。あなた
はあの日、私の命を助けてくれました。だから恩
返しがしたかったのです。あなたを助けることで。
だから、私は人になりました。そして、あなたの
妻になれて、とても幸せでした。あなたを心から
お慕いしていました。あなたが食べていくために
お金がいるというから、私は羽を折って反物を織
りました。でもあなたはもっとお金がほしくなっ
て……」

"Yes," said his wife. "I'm the crane. You saved my life that day, and I wanted to give back. I wanted to help you in return. So I became human...I was happy as your wife, and I learned to love you very much. When you said you needed money for food, I used my feathers to weave the cloth. But then you wanted *more* money..."

　「大切な妻よ」若者はそう言うと泣きだしました。「私は知らなかった。もしわかっていれば……」

　「私はあなたとずっと一緒にいたかった。でもあなたは私の秘密を知ってしまいました。それはあってはならないこと。私はここを去らなければなりません」

　「いやだ！」若者は妻のあとを追って、玄関に行きます。「どうか、ここにいてくれないか。お金なんかどうでもいい。お前がいてくれればいいのだよ」

　妻は外に出て、悲しげに振りかえります。

　「お許しください。これはあってはならないことなのです」

　すると、若者の目のまえで、妻は白い鶴になり、翼を広げて空に飛びたちます。

　鶴は一度若者のうえをまわると、また悲しそうな声で鳴きました。そして、そのまま雲のなかへと飛んでゆき、二度と若者のまえに姿を見せることはありませんでした。

"My dear wife!" cried the young man. "I didn't know! If I—"

"My hope was to stay with you forever," his wife said. "But now that you know my secret, it is not to be. I must leave you."

"No!" The young man followed his wife to the front door. "Please don't leave! I don't need money! I only want you!"

His wife stepped outside and turned to look at him sadly.

"I'm sorry," she said. "It is not to be."

And then, right before his eyes, she turned back into a white crane.

The crane spread her wings and rose up into the air. She circled once in the sky above the young man and let out another sad cry. Then she flew off into the clouds, and he never saw her again.

The Mouse's
Wedding

ねずみの嫁入り

　これは、ねずみについての古いお話です。

　昔々、あるところに、とてもかわいらしい若いねずみが住んでいました。そして、両親はいつも、「世界一すてきな男を娘のために見つけなければ」と言っていました。

　ある日、お父さんはお母さんに言いました。「お母さんよ。太陽こそがもっともすてきだよ。だって、我々を照らして、明かりをくれるのだから」

　二人は太陽のところに行って頼みました。「太陽さん。あなたは世界で最もすてきな男ですよね。どうか娘と結婚してくれませんか」

　太陽は答えます。「うーむ。ねずみさん。私は世界で最もすてきな男じゃないよ。最もすてきなのは雲だよ。だって、雲はいつも私を遮るのだから」

　「なるほど」お父さんはそう言うと、
　二人で雲をたずねます。「雲さん。あなたは世界

This is an old story about a mouse.

Long, long ago there was a beautiful young mouse. The parents were always saying, "We must look for the most wonderful man in the world for our daughter."

One day the father said to his wife, "Mother, it is the sun that is the most wonderful, because it shines over us and gives us light."

They went to the sun and asked him, "Mr. Sun, you are the most wonderful man in the world, aren't you? Will you marry our daughter?"

The sun answered, "Well, Mr. Mouse, I am not the most wonderful man in the world. It is the cloud that is the most wonderful, because he covers me all the time."

"Oh, I see," said the father.

They went to the cloud and asked him,

で最もすてきな男ですよね。どうか娘と結婚して
くれませんか」

　すると雲は言いました。「うーむ。ねずみさん。
私は世界で最もすてきな男じゃないよ。最もすて
きなのは風だよ。だって、風は私を吹き飛ばすの
だから」
　「なるほど」お父さんはそう言うと、
　二人で風をたずねます。「風さん。あなたは世界
で最もすてきな男ですよね。どうか娘と結婚して
くれませんか」

　すると風は答えます。「うーむ。ねずみさん。私
は世界で最もすてきな男じゃないよ。最もすてき
なのは壁だよ。だって、壁は私を止めることがで
きるのだから」
　「なるほど」お父さんはそう言うと、
　二人で壁をたずねます。「壁さん。あなたは世界
で最もすてきな男ですよね。どうか娘と結婚して
くれませんか」

　すると壁は答えます。「うーむ。ねずみさん。私

"Mr. Cloud, you are the most wonderful man in the world, aren't you? Will you marry our daughter?"

The cloud answered, "Well, Mr. Mouse, I am not the most wonderful man in the world. It is the wind that is the most wonderful, because he can blow me away."

"Oh, I see," said the father.

They went to the wind and asked him, "Mr. Wind, you are the most wonderful man in the world, aren't you? Will you marry our daughter?"

The wind answered, "Well, Mr. Mouse, I am not the most wonderful man in the world. It is the wall that is the most wonderful, because he can stop me."

"Oh, I see," said the father.

They went to the wall and asked him, "Mr. Wall, you are the most wonderful man in the world, aren't you? Will you marry our daughter?"

The wall answered, "Well, Mr. Mouse, I

は世界で最もすてきな男じゃないよ。最もすてき
なのはねずみだよ。だって、ねずみは私をかじる
のだから」

「なるほど」お父さんはそう言うと、

娘に近くに住んでいるすてきな若いねずみと結
婚するように言いました。

「ああ、あなたは世界で最もすてきな男。どうか
娘と結婚してくださいませんか」と二人は言いまし
た。

「よろこんで」若いねずみは言いました。

お父さんもお母さんもとても満足。やがて二人
にはたくさんの孫ができたのでした。

am not the most wonderful man in the world. It is the mouse that is the most wonderful, because he can eat me."

"Oh, I see," said the father.

The parents decided to ask their daughter to marry a nice young mouse who lived near them.

"Oh, you are the most wonderful man in the world. Would you marry our daughter?" they said.

"I would be happy to," he said.

Both the father and his wife were very happy. Soon they had many grandchildren.

The Old Man with
a Lump

こぶとりじいさん

こぶとりじいさん

　昔々のこと、頬に大きなこぶのあるおじいさん
がいました。ある日おじいさんは山に薪をとりに
行きました。すると、いきなり雨が降りだしたので、
おじいさんは山にある小さなお寺で雨やどり。

　おじいさんは、そこで眠ってしまいました。気
がつくと、お寺の外でたくさんの赤鬼や青鬼が踊
ったり、お酒をのんだりして騒いでいるではあり
ませんか。おじいさんは踊りが大好き。一緒に踊
りたくなってしまいました。
　おじいさんは鬼たちと一緒に踊っても怖くあり
ません。鬼たちはおじいさんの踊りをとても気に
いりました。
　朝がきて、鬼の頭が言いました。「おまえはとて
も踊りがじょうずだな。明日の夜もここに来い。
それまでおまえの大切なこぶを預かっておいてや
る」鬼は言いおわると、おじいさんのこぶを取って
しまったのです。

Long, long ago there lived an old man who had a lump on his cheek. One day he went to a mountain to find firewood. It suddenly began to rain, so he went to a small temple on the mountain to stay dry.

He slept until he heard some music outside the temple. There were many red and blue demons dancing, drinking and enjoying themselves. He felt like dancing himself because he liked it very much.

He forgot to be afraid and joined the group of dancing demons. All the demons enjoyed his wonderful dancing.

When it became light in the morning, the leader of the demons said to him, "You are a wonderful dancer. You can come tomorrow night. Until that time, I will keep your important lump." The demon took his lump away.

　おじいさんが家に帰っておばあさんにその話を
していると、隣のいじわるじいさんがそれを盗み
ぎきしたのです。

　いじわるじいさんにもこぶがありました。そこ
で、いじわるじいさんは、こぶを取られた正直じ
いさんよりも先にお寺に行って、鬼の来るのを待
っていました。

　間もなく、たくさんの鬼が踊りをはじめました。
いじわるじいさんは、鬼が怖くてしかたありませ
ん。しかし、こぶを取ってもらいたいので、踊り
はじめました。ところが、いじわるじいさんの踊
りと歌はとてもひどいものでした。

　鬼たちはとても怒って、正直じいさんのこぶを
いじわるじいさんのもう片方の頬にくっつけたと
いうことです。

When he returned home and told his old wife the story, the mean old man next door listened to what he said.

The mean old man had a lump, too, and that night he went to the temple before the nice old man and waited for the time to come.

Soon many demons began to dance. He was very afraid of demons, but he wanted to have his lump taken away, so he started to dance. But his dancing and singing were very poor.

The demons got very angry and put the nice man's lump on his other cheek.

Kachi Kachi
Mountain

かちかち山

かちかち山

　昔々、あるところに、年老いたお百姓のおじい
さんとおばあさんが住んでいました。
　毎日、おじいさんは、畑に行きます。畑仕事は
大変でした。ところが、裏山から狸がやってきて、
おじいさんの仕事をもっと難しくしてしまいます。
　狸は昔から、いたずらをすることで知られてい
ます。この裏山の狸も毎日のように、おじいさん
に意地悪をするのです。

　その日、お百姓のおじいさんは種を植えていま
した。
　「小さな種よ、たくさんの食べものになっておく
れ」おじいさんは、一粒一粒種を土に入れるたびに、
そう歌います。

*

　昼におじいさんは家でお昼ご飯を食べました。
おじいさんがご飯を食べているあいだに、狸は畑
にやってきて、種をすべて掘りおこし、食べてし

Long, long ago, an old farmer and his wife lived in a certain place.

Each day the farmer worked hard in his field. And each day a tanuki from the Mountain in Back made his work even harder.

A tanuki looks like a cross between a raccoon and a dog. This animal is famous in Japan for playing tricks on people. And the tanuki from the Mountain in Back was always causing trouble for the old farmer.

Today the farmer was planting.

"One little seed, a hundred meals!" he sang as he pushed each seed into the ground.

*

At noon he went inside the house for lunch. And while he was gone, the tanuki ran through the field, dug up all the seeds,

まったのです。お百姓のおじいさんが仕事をしに
もどってきたとき、狸を見つけ怒鳴りつけます。

「この悪者め。ここから出てゆけ！」

「たくさんの種が、ちょっとの食事」狸はそう言
って笑うと、薮の中に走ってゆきました。

おじいさんはとても腹がたちました。おじいさ
んは動物が好きですが、このやり方はあんまりで
す。おじいさんは午後をついやして、罠をつくり
ます。

*

狸は、人にいろいろと迷惑をかけますが、あま
り利口ではありません。その次の日の朝、お百姓
のおじいさんが罠を見にゆくと、やっぱり。そこ
に狸がひっかかっているではありませんか。おじ
いさんは、狸の四本の足をしっかりと縄でくくり、
家に運ぶと、縄の端を台所の梁にくくりつけます。

「ついにこの悪い狸を捕まえた」おじいさんはお
ばあさんに言いました。「ちゃんと見はっていてく
れよ。こいつのいたずらにひっかからないように。
今夜は狸汁を食べようか」

and ate them. When the farmer came back outside, he saw the tanuki and shouted:

"You little devil! Get out of my field!"

"A hundred seeds, one little meal!" the tanuki laughed and ran off into the brush.

The farmer was very angry. He loved animals, but enough was enough. He spent the rest of the afternoon making a trap.

*

The tanuki was good at causing trouble, but he was not very bright. The next morning, the farmer went to check his trap. And, sure enough, there was the tanuki. He was hanging by all four feet at the end of a rope. The farmer carried him into the house and tied the other end of the rope to the kitchen rafters.

"I finally caught this bad tanuki," he told his wife. "Keep an eye on him, and don't fall for any of his tricks. I want tanuki soup for dinner!"

「そうしましょう」おばあさんは言いました。

　おじいさんが畑にもどってゆくと、おばあさん
は家のまわりで仕事をはじめます。狸は何もしゃ
べりません。ただ、じっとおばあさんの動きを見
ています。

　しばらくして、おばあさんは、台所にきてきび
を臼にいれました。きび餅を狸汁に入れようと思
ったのです。おばあさんが、きびを挽(ひ)くために重
い木づちを持ちあげたとき、狸はようやく口を開
きます。

　「おばあさん」その声は悲しそうです。「ごめんな
さい。私は悪い狸でした。せめて死ぬ前に一つよ
い事がしたいのです。おばあさんの手つだいをさ
せてください。この木づちはあなたのようなお年
よりにはとても重いはずですから」

　「嘘をつくんじゃないよ」

　おばあさんがそう言うと、「嘘なんか、つきませ
ん。おばあさん。私は喜んでおばあさんとおじい
さんのために狸汁になりましょう。でも、この世
を去る前に一つだけよい事がしたいのです」そう狸
は懇願します。

"Very well, dear," she said.

When the farmer went back out to his field, the old woman began working around the house. The tanuki didn't say a word. But his eyes followed her every move.

After a while, the old woman went into the kitchen and put some millet in the mortar. She wanted to make millet cakes to go with the tanuki soup. When she picked up the heavy wooden mallet, to pound the millet, the tanuki finally spoke.

"Grandmother," he said in a sad voice. "I'm sorry I've been such a bad tanuki. I want to do just one good thing before I die. Please let me help you. That mallet is much too heavy for an old woman like you!"

"You can't fool me," the old woman said.

"I'm not trying to fool you, Grandmother," the tanuki said. "I'm happy to be soup for you and the good farmer. But just once, before I leave this life, I want to do the right thing!"

　おばあさんは心の優しい人でした。結局狸を信じてしまい、縄をほどいて重たい木づちを手わたします。しかし、狸は木づちを使っておばあさんを助けるどころか、なんとそれを高々と持ちあげて、おばあさんの頭の真うえから振りおろしたのです。

*

　その日の午後おそく、おじいさんが家にもどってきました。おなかが空いていたので、狸汁を楽しみにして。ところがそこで見たものは……。なんとおばあさんが死んで、狸はどこかに行っているではありませんか。

　おじいさんは家の入りぐちに座りこみ、悲嘆にくれます。どうしていいかわかりません。おじいさんがそこに座りこんでいると、かわいらしいうさぎが前の山からやってきました。うさぎはおじいさんの仲のいい友だちです。

　「どうしたの。おじいさん」うさぎはたずねます。

　お百姓さんは、ことのすべてをうさぎに話してきかせました。涙が頬をつたって流れます。うさぎも一緒に泣きました。

The old woman had a soft heart, and in the end she believed the tanuki. She untied him and handed him the heavy wooden mallet. But he didn't use the mallet to help the old woman. He lifted it high in the air and brought it right down on her head!

*

Late that afternoon, the farmer came back home. He was hungry and looking forward to his tanuki soup. But what did he find? His dear wife was dead on the floor, and the tanuki was gone.

The old farmer sat down on the front step. His heart was broken, and he didn't know what to do. He was still sitting there, when the cute little rabbit from the Mountain in Front came along. This rabbit was a close friend.

"What's wrong, Grandfather?" she said.

The farmer told her the whole story. Tears were running down his face. The rabbit cried too.

「ひどい狸ね！　心配しないでおじいさん、きっと敵はとってあげるからね」

*

　次の日になりました。うさぎは裏山にのぼってゆきました。かごに薪をたくさん入れて。うさぎは狸の穴のそばに座って、栗の実を食べながらひとやすみ。

　栗のにおいをかいで、狸は穴から出てきました。

「うさぎ。お前何を食べている」狸はたずねます。
「栗の実よ」
「少し、おくれよ」
「どうぞ」うさぎは応えます。「でも、その前に手つだって。この薪を運んでくれない？　私にはとても重くて」
「もちろん」
　狸はそう言うと、薪の入ったかごを背中に担いで山をおりはじめます。うさぎはうしろからついてきます。そして、火打石を打ちはじめました。カチッ、カチッ！　うさぎはかごの薪に火をつけよ

"That terrible tanuki!" she said. "Don't worry, Grandfather. He won't get away with this!"

*

The next day, the rabbit walked up the Mountain in Back. As she walked, she filled her basket with pieces of wood. She sat down to rest near the tanuki's hole and began eating chestnuts.

The tanuki smelled the chestnuts and came outside.

"What are you eating, Rabbit?" he said.

"Chestnuts."

"Can I have some?"

"Yes," said the rabbit. "But please help me first. Can you carry this wood? It's so heavy for me..."

"Gladly!" said the tanuki.

He tied the basket of wood to his back and started down the mountain. The rabbit followed behind him. Soon she began hitting two rocks together: *Kachi! Kachi!* She was

うとしているのです。

「おいうさぎ。そのカチッ、カチッって音は何の音だ？」狸はききます。

「別に。ただ、カチカチ山からきたカチカチ鳥がいるだけよ」

「なるほど。俺さまもそんなことは知ってたよ」狸はそう言いました。

trying to set the basket of wood on fire.

"Say, Rabbit," said the tanuki. "What's that 'kachi, kachi' sound?"

"Oh, that's nothing," said the rabbit. "It's just the Kachi Kachi Bird from Kachi Kachi Mountain."

"Oh, right," said the tanuki. "I already knew that."

　やがて火打石の火の粉が薪に移り、薪は燃えてパチパチと音をたてます。

　「おいうさぎ。このパチパチって音は何の音だ？」

　「別に。ただ、パチパチ山からきたパチパチ鳥がいるだけよ」

　「なるほど。俺さまもそんなことは知ってたよ」

　しばらくすると、狸の背中が熱くなります。

「おいうさぎ。いやに暑くないかい、今日は？」
誰もそれには応えません。
「おいうさぎ」
　狸は振りかえりますが、うさぎはどこにもいませんでした。でもそこに火が。
　「助けてくれ！」狸は叫びます。「燃えちゃうよ！」
　狸はおお急ぎで川に向かって走りだします。

＊

Soon a spark from the rocks landed on the wood, and the wood started burning. It crackled as it burned.

"Say, Rabbit, what's that 'crackle, crackle' sound?"

"Oh, that's nothing. It's just the Crackle Crackle Bird from Crackle Crackle Mountain."

"Oh, right," said the tanuki. "I already knew that."

After a while, he began to feel the heat of the fire on his back.

"Say, Rabbit, it's hot today, isn't it?"

There was no answer.

"Rabbit?"

The tanuki turned to look back. He didn't see the rabbit, but he saw the fire.

"Help!" he shouted. "I'm burning!"

And he ran toward the river as fast as he could go.

*

　さらにその次の日、うさぎは裏山にもどってきます。練った唐辛子をいっぱいかごに入れて。狸は穴から出て、うさぎを呼びとめます。

　「昨日はどこに行ったんだ。うさぎ」狸は言います。「薪に火がついて、俺の背中の毛を焼いてしまった。痛いじゃないか」
　「薬をとりに行ったのよ。やけどにきく薬をね」とうさぎは答えます。
　「そうか。それを背中につけてくれ」狸はそう言いました。
　「向こうを向いて」うさぎはそう言うと、狸のやけどのあとに、練った唐辛子をしっかりと塗りつけます。
　「おー！　熱々！」狸は叫びます。

　「我慢しなさい。明日にはよくなっているわ」うさぎはそう言うと、急いで山にもどります。

*

The next day, the rabbit returned to the Mountain in Back. She was carrying a bag full of red hot pepper paste. The tanuki came out of his hole and stopped her.

"Where did you go yesterday, Rabbit?" he said. "The wood caught fire! It burned all the hair off my back! It hurts!"

"I went to get this medicine," said the rabbit. "It's the best thing for burns."

"Oh, please put it on my back!" said the tanuki.

"Turn around," the rabbit said. She painted a thick coat of pepper paste on the tanuki's burns.

"OH!" shouted the tanuki. "OH! THAT'S HOT!"

"Be strong," the rabbit said and smiled. "I'm sure you'll feel better tomorrow."

And she hurried back down the mountain.

*

　そして、その次の朝、狸はうさぎが川におりて
ゆくのを見つけます。うさぎは木を使って舟をつ
くっていたのです。
「狸さん！　少しはよくなった？」

「ああ、まあね。でも昨日の夜はとても痛かった」

「それはよかったわ」
「何をやってるんだ」狸はたずねます。

「舟をつくってるの」
「なぜ」
「だって、川の真んなかで大きなお魚を捕まえた
いの」
「そうか。俺も大きな魚がほしい。舟をつくって
いいかい」
「もちろん」うさぎは応えます。「でもあなたは私
より重いわね。泥で舟をつくらなきゃ」

「なるほど。俺さまもそんなことは知ってたよ」
そう狸は言いました。
　そして狸は川岸の泥をとって舟をつくります。

The next morning, the tanuki found the rabbit down by the river. She was building a boat out of wood.

"Hello, Tanuki!" she said. "Do you feel better today?"

"I guess so," said the tanuki. "But last night I was in such pain!"

"That's good," said the rabbit.

"What are you doing?" the tanuki asked her.

"I'm building a boat."

"How come?"

"Well, I want to catch the big fish in the middle of the river."

"Oh! I want some big fish too! Can I build a boat?"

"Sure," said the rabbit. "But you're much heavier than I am. You should make your boat out of mud."

"Oh, right," said the tanuki. "I already knew that."

So the tanuki took mud from the bank of

それは大きなお椀のような舟でした。うさぎと狸
は舟ができあがると、さっそく川の真んなかまで
漕いでいきます。そこの水は冷たくて、とても深
いのに、狸のどろ舟は、壊れはじめます。

　「助けてくれ！」狸は叫びます。「うさぎ、助けて。
俺は泳げないんだ！」

　しかし、うさぎは木でつくった舟をあやつって
岸へと引き返すだけ。

the river and made a boat. It was shaped like a big bowl. When both boats were finished, the rabbit and the tanuki rode them out to the middle of the river. The water was cold and deep there, and the tanuki's boat of mud began to fall to pieces.

"Help!" he shouted. "Rabbit, save me! I can't swim!"

But the rabbit just turned her wood boat around and headed for land.

　うさぎがお百姓のおじいさんの家に帰ってきたとき、すでに日も暮れかけていました。おじいさんは家の入りぐちに座っています。

「あの狸はもう誰にも悪さはできないわ」

　おじいさんは何も言わず、手をうさぎの頭にのせました。そして一緒に太陽が沈んでいくのを見るのでした。

The sun was low in the sky when she got back to the old farmer's house. The farmer was sitting on the front step.

"That tanuki will never hurt anyone again," she told him.

The old man said nothing, but put his hand on the rabbit's head. And together they watched the sun go down.

The Bamboo
Princess

かぐや姫

　昔々、おじいさんとおばあさんがとある村に住んでいました。二人は竹を切って、籠^{かご}やいろいろなものをつくって暮らしていました。

　ある日、おじいさんはいつものように森に行くと、輝く竹を見つけました。おじいさんがその竹を切ってなかを見ると、驚いたことに女の赤ちゃんがそこにいるではありませんか。

　おじいさんとおばあさんには子どもがいません。そこでその赤ちゃんを引き取ってかぐや姫と名づけました。それからというもの、おじいさんが竹を切るとそこにはいつも小判が入っています。やがて一家はお金持ちになりした。そしてかぐや姫は日を追うごとに育っていって、とても美しい娘になりました。その噂を聞いて、多くの男たちがあちこちからたずねてきて、かぐや姫をお嫁にもらおうとします。でも、かぐや姫は誰にも興味を示しません。

Long, long ago there lived an old man and his wife in a village. They cut bamboo and made baskets and other things out of it to get money.

One day the man went to the forest as always, and he found a shining bamboo plant. He cut it open, and to his surprise, he found a baby girl inside.

The old man and his wife had no children of their own, so they took her in and named her *Kaguya Hime* (Bamboo Princess). Every time the man went to cut bamboo after that, he found money in it. Soon he and his family became rich. Kaguya Hime grew day by day to be a very beautiful lady. Hearing of her beauty, many young men from various places visited her house because they wanted to marry her. But she never showed any interest in them.

　かぐや姫はいつも何か他のことを考えているようで、ただ空を見つめています。

　おじいさんは、たびたびたずねてくる男たちを放っておくわけにもいきません。そこで、男たちに、この世で最もすてきな宝物を持ってきた者に、かぐや姫をお嫁にやると約束したのです。

　何人かの男たちがとてもすてきな宝物を持ってきました。しかし、かぐや姫はそのどれにも満足ではありません。

　やがて、かぐや姫は月を見るたびに泣くようになりました。

　「どうしてそんなに悲しいのかい。何があったのかね」おじいさんはたずねました。

　「大丈夫です。私の話を聞いてください。実は私は月で生まれたのです。そして中秋の名月のときに、使いが迎えにきて、月に帰らなければならないのです」

　「なんということだ」おじいさんはびっくり。中秋の名月は明日ではありませんか。

　おじいさんは、さむらいたちにお願いして、使

She always looked like she was thinking about something else, and just looked up at the sky.

Her father could not ignore the men who were always visiting, so he told them that the man who brought the greatest treasure in the world would be able to marry her.

Some of the men brought wonderful treasures, but she always said that they were not special enough.

Soon she began to cry every time she saw the moon.

"What makes you so sad? What's the matter?" asked the father.

"I am all right. Listen to me. I was born on the moon. I must return to the moon on the night of the 15th of August, when some visitors are coming to pick me up."

"That is crazy," said the father. He was very angry. The 15th of August was the next day.

The father found a group of samurai to

者からかぐや姫を守ろうとします。かぐや姫が月に帰らないようにと心で祈りながら。

　その夜、月が山から上ったとき、いきなりまぶしい明かりがおじいさんの家にいる男たちに降りそそぎます。さむらいたちは、月に向かって矢を放ちました。しかし、何にもあたりません。そして、もっと明るく光ったとき、さむらいたちは、眠ってしまいました。

keep her safe from the visitors. He hoped that she would never return to the moon.

That night, as the moon was rising over the mountains, its light suddenly flashed down on the men at the old man's house. Many of them shot arrows at the moon, but none of them could hit it. Then, there was a bright flash of light, and they all began to sleep.

　月のお使いが、光に乗って、家におりてきます。
かぐや姫は光に向かって動かずにはいられません。
お使いに手をとられてゆっくりと空へとあがって
ゆきます。誰もそれを止めることはできませんで
した。
　おじいさんも、おばあさんも、ただその様子を
眺めているだけでした。

An angel came down through the light from the moon to the house. Kaguya Hime could not help moving toward the light. She slowly flew up to the sky hand-in-hand with the angel. Nothing could stop them.

The old man and his wife could do nothing as they watched her return to the moon.

A Tiger
on a Paper Screen

一休さん
──屏風の虎退治

　昔々、京都に、一休禅師という賢いお坊さんが
いました。これは一休さんが子どもだった頃のお
話です。

　あるえらい殿さまが一休さんのうわさを聞き、
一休さんを試そうと思いました。「実は困ったこと
があり、お前の知恵を借りたいのじゃ」殿さまはそ
う言って、虎の絵が描かれた屏風を一休さんに見
せました。
　「この大きな虎にはほとほと困っておる。ときど
き夜中に屏風から抜け出してわしらを驚かせるの
じゃ。虎が屏風から出てきたら、捕まえて縄でし
ばってくれぬか」

　一休さんは驚きました。しばらく考えてから言
いました。「わかりました。やってみましょう。お
殿さま、虎をしばる丈夫な縄をくださいませ」一休
さんは殿さまから縄をもらい、虎を捕まえようと
屏風の前に立ちました。

Long, long ago, there was a wise Buddhist priest named Ikkyu Zenji, who lived in Kyoto. This is a story about when he was a child.

A great lord heard about his wisdom and decided to test him. "I have a problem I'd like you to help me with," said the lord. He showed Ikkyu a paper screen with a picture of a tiger painted on it.

"We're having trouble with this big tiger. It sometimes comes off the screen and surprises us at night. I want you to catch and tie the tiger with a rope when it comes off the screen."

Ikkyu was surprised. After thinking a little, he said, "Well, okay. I'll do it. My Lord, would you give me a strong rope to catch the tiger with?" The lord gave him a rope, and Ikkyu stood in front of the screen to catch the tiger.

「お殿さま、屏風の前にお立ちになってはあぶのうございます。屏風の後ろに回り、虎を追い出してくださいませ」一休さんは言いました。

「何だと？　わしに虎を屏風から追い出せと言うのか」殿さまは言いました。

「そうです、お殿さま。虎を追い出すことができなければ、縄でしばることはできませんから」一休さんは言いました。

「それは無理じゃ」殿さまは言いました。一休さんが本当に賢いということがよくわかったようです。

Ikkyu said, "My Lord. It's very dangerous to stand in front of the screen. Why don't you go behind the screen and drive the tiger out of it?"

"What? Are you saying I should drive the tiger out of the screen?" asked the lord.

Ikkyu said, "Yes, My Lord. If you can't drive the tiger out, I can't catch it with a rope."

"I can't do that," said the lord. The lord realized that Ikkyu was a very wise boy.

The Snow Lady

雪女

雪女

　昔々、遠い北の国に、一人の若者とその父親が
住んでいました。ある雪の降る日、二人は山へ出
かけました。天気が急に悪くなったので、山小屋
で一晩過ごし、天気が良くなるのを待つことにし
ました。

　真夜中、戸が開く大きな音がして目を覚ますと、
そこには見知らぬ女が立っていました。若者は女
に話しかけようとしましたが、女は父親に冷たい
息を吹きかけました。すると父親は白い氷になっ
てしまいました。「この女は雪の精にちがいない」
若者はそう思いました。

　「あなたはまだ若いので助けてあげましょう。で
も、このことは決してだれにも話してはなりませ
ん！」雪の精はそう言って、雪の中に消えていきま
した。翌朝目を覚ますと、父親は死んでいました。

Long, long ago, there lived a young man and his father in the far north. One snowy day, they went to the mountains. The weather suddenly became bad, so they decided to stay the night in a mountain hut and wait for the weather to get better.

In the middle of the night, the door opened with a loud sound and woke them up. They saw a strange woman standing there. The young man was about to speak to her, but she breathed cold air on his father, and he froze and turned white. The young man thought to himself, "She must be a snow spirit."

The spirit said to him, "You are young, so I'll help you. But never tell anyone about this!" She disappeared into the snow. The next morning when he woke up, his father was dead.

　それから一年が過ぎ、ある雨の日のこと、若者は家の軒下で美しい娘が雨宿りをしているのを見かけました。やさしい若者は娘を家に招き入れ、娘の話を聞いてやりました。娘の名はおゆきといい、身よりはいませんでした。まもなく、二人はお互いのことが好きになり、夫婦になりました。二人の子どもに恵まれ、幸せに暮らしていました。

　ある雪の降る日のこと、男は妻に雪の精の話をしました。すると、妻はとても悲しそうな顔をしました。「とうとう話してしまったのですね。決して話してはならないと私が言ったのを忘れたのですか」そう言って外へ飛び出しました。妻は雪の精だったのです。もう人の姿では生きていけません。

　「おゆき！　おゆき！」男は叫びましたが、おゆきは二度と戻ってきませんでした。

About one year later, on a rainy day, the man found a beautiful lady standing under the eaves of his house waiting for the rain to stop. He was a kind young man, and he invited her into his house to hear her story. Her name was Oyuki, which means snow. She had no family to help her. Soon, they fell in love with each other and got married. They had two children, and they were very happy.

One snowy night, the man told his wife about the snow spirit. She became very sad and said, "You finally decided to talk about it. Don't you remember that I said you should never do that?" She ran outside. She was the snow spirit. She could no longer live in the body of a human being.

He cried, "Oyuki, Oyuki!" but she was gone.

Grandfather
Flowers

花咲かじいさん

　昔々、ある小さな村に、とても親切なおじいさんとおばあさんが住んでいました。でも、そのお似合いの二人には残念なことに子どもがいません。そんな二人は一匹の犬をとても大事にしていました。白い犬だったので、シロと名づけられ、二人は自分の息子のようにシロをかわいがっていました。

　ところで、その隣には、もう一組のおじいさんとおばあさんが住んでいました。でもその二人はあまり良い人たちではありません。二人はよく張りで意地悪で、自分たちのことしか考えていません。そして、二人はお隣が嫌いで、シロのことも嫌いでした。かわいそうに、時々二人はシロに石を投げたりさえしていました。

　ある日、いつものように、親切なおじいさんは畑で仕事をしていました。シロも、おじいさんといっしょ。地面に鍬をいれているあいだ、シロは走りまわって、あちこちクンクンとにおいをかいでまわります。突然、シロが畑の角にある大きな

Long, long ago, a kind old man and woman lived in a little village somewhere. Sadly, these nice old people had no children. But they had a dog they loved very much. The dog was white, and his name was Shiro. Shiro was almost like a son to the kind old couple.

Now, another old man and woman lived next door. And this old man and woman were not so nice. In fact, they were greedy and mean. They cared only about themselves, and they didn't like their neighbors. They didn't like Shiro, either. Sometimes they even threw rocks at the poor dog.

One day, as always, the kind old man went out to work in his field. Shiro went with him. The old man turned the ground with his hoe, while Shiro ran around and enjoyed all the different smells. Suddenly Shiro stopped in

木のしたで止まって吠えはじめました。

「ここ掘れワンワン。ここだよ」
「どうしたシロ」
　親切なおじいさんはシロのまえの土を掘ってみ
ます。すると鍬がなにか固いものにぶつかります。
それは重い木の箱でした。なんと、驚いたことに、
箱は小判でいっぱいでした。

one corner of the field, under a big tree, and started to bark.

"Hoe here! *Arf! Arf!* Hoe here!"

"What is it, Shiro?"

When the kind old man dug into the ground in front of Shiro, his hoe hit something hard. It was a heavy wooden box. And, to the old man's great surprise, the box was full of gold coins!

　シロのおかげで、親切なおじいさんとおばあさんはお金持ちになりました。お隣のいじわるじいさんは、そのことが面白くありません。もちろんいじわるばあさんも同じです。

　「なんであんな愚かな年よりが良いめにあうのじゃ」いじわるばあさんはじいさんに言いました。「あの犬をさらっておいで、わしらにも宝を見つけてくれるに違いない」

　「それはいい」いじわるじいさんは言いました。いじわるじいさんは、隣に行って、シロの首に縄をつけて、かわいそうに、むりやり自分の畑につれてゆきました。

　「ここにも宝があるはずじゃ。探さんかい！」

　縄はシロの首をしめるので、ついにシロは悲鳴をあげて、倒れこみます。

　「ここじゃな？」いじわるじいさんは、そこを掘って掘って、ついに柔らかい泥まで鍬をいれました。いじわるじいさんは、両手でそれをすくいますが、そこには黄金はありません。そこにあったのは泥とゴミ、そして小さな虫ども。ひどい臭いがしているではありませんか。

Thanks to Shiro, the kind old man and woman were now rich. When the mean old man next door heard about this, he was not happy. His wife wasn't happy either.

"Why should those old fools have all the luck?" she said to her husband. "Go get that dog! He can find some treasure for us too!"

"Good idea," said the mean old man. He marched right next door, tied a rope around Shiro's neck, and pulled the poor dog out to his field.

"There must be treasure here too," he said. "Find it!"

The rope hurt Shiro's neck, and finally he let out a cry and fell down.

"This is the place, is it?" the mean old man said and started digging. He dug and dug, and finally he broke through to soft mud. He reached in with both hands, but he didn't find any gold—just mud and waste and strange little bugs. A terrible smell filled the air.

　いじわるじいさんは、とても腹をたて、地団駄を踏んで、シロを叱りつけます。そしてついに鍬を手にとりました。いじわるじいさんは、鍬を振りあげて、思いきりシロの頭をたたいたのです。かわいそうなシロは一哭（な）きすると、死んでしまいました。

*

　親切なおじいさんとおばあさんはそのことを知ると、とても悲しみました。二人とも泣きながら、死んでしまったシロを家につれて帰りました。そして、庭の角に、シロの墓をつくって、そこに埋葬したのです。そしてお墓のうえにちいさな松を植えたのです。

　すると何がおこったと思います？　なんと木が二人の目のまえで、どんどん大きくなるではありませんか。どんどん伸びて、家より高く、手を伸ばしても抱きかかえられないほど大きくなりました。

　「これはシロの贈りものじゃ」親切なおじいさんは言いました。「この木を使えば、これから死ぬまで料理をしたり、暖をとったりできる。幹を使えばきっとすばらしい臼ができる」

The mean old man was very angry. He jumped up and down and shouted at Shiro, and finally he picked up his hoe. He lifted it over the poor dog's head and brought it down as hard as he could. Shiro gave one little cry and died.

*

When the kind old man and woman found out about this, they were very sad. Both of them cried as they carried Shiro's body home. They dug a grave for him in one corner of their garden. Then they planted a little pine tree on top of the grave.

And what do you think happened next? The tree began to grow, right before their eyes. It grew and grew and grew, until it was taller than the house and too big to reach around.

"It's a present from Shiro!" the kind old man said. "With all this wood, we can cook and keep warm for the rest of our lives. And what a beautiful mortar the trunk will make!"

「そうですね。臼をつくってくださいな、おじいさん」親切なおばあさんは言いました。「それでお餅をつくりましょう。シロがとても好きだったお餅を」

そこで、おじいさんは木を倒して、幹から臼をつくりました。臼ができると、おじいさんはそれを台所にもってゆきます。おばあさんがお米を臼にいれて二人はそれぞれに杵を手にとります。

「これはシロへの贈りもの」二人はそう言って、餅つきをはじめました。すると何がおこったと思いますか？ 杵を持ち上げるたびに臼のお米が増えていくのです。あっという間に、臼はお米でいっぱいに。それでもお米が湧いてきます。まもなく台所はお米でいっぱいになったのです。

「これはシロからの贈りものじゃ。これでわしらはずっと食べていける」親切なおばあさんは言いました。

*

お隣のいじわるばあさんはその話を聞くと、とても腹をたてました。いじわるじいさんも一緒です。

"Oh, yes! Please make a mortar, dear," said the kind old woman. "We can use it to prepare rice cakes. Shiro always loved rice cakes!"

So the old man cut the tree down and made a mortar out of the trunk. When it was ready, he brought it into the kitchen. The old woman put some rice in the bowl of the mortar, and they each picked up a mallet.

"This is for you, Shiro!" they said and began pounding the rice. And what do you think happened? Each time they lifted their mallets, they saw more rice in the mortar. In no time at all, the mortar was full, and still the rice kept coming. Soon the whole kitchen was filled with rice.

"It's a present from Shiro!" said the kind old woman. "Now we'll never be hungry again!"

*

When the mean old woman next door heard about this, she was very angry. Her husband was angry too.

「なんであんな愚かな年よりばかりが良いめにあうのじゃ」じいさんは続けます。「あの臼をもらってくることにしよう」

じいさんは隣に行って臼を取りあげると、それを家に転がしてゆきました。そして台所において、いじわるばあさんがお米をそこに入れました。そして二人は杵を振りあげて、餅つきをはじめたのです。するとまもなく、臼は泥やゴミ、そして小さな虫たちでいっぱいになったのです。家中がひどい臭いに包まれます。

いじわるじいさんといじわるばあさんは、とても腹をたて、地団駄を踏んで怒鳴ります。そしてついにいじわるじいさんは斧をとって臼を切りきざみ、火のなかに放りこみました。

親切なおじいさんが臼を返してもらいにくると、そこにはただ灰があるだけ。おじいさんは籠いっぱいに灰をいれると、悲しみながらそれを家に持って帰りました。

「灰をシロの墓にまいてやりましょう」おばあさんはそう言いました。

"Why should those old fools have all the luck?" he said. "I'm going to borrow that mortar!"

And he marched right next door, turned the mortar over, and rolled it to his house. He set it up in the kitchen, and his wife put some rice in the bowl. Then they both picked up mallets and started pounding. And in no time at all, the mortar was full—of mud and waste and strange little bugs! A terrible smell filled the house.

The mean old couple were very angry. They jumped up and down and shouted, and finally the mean old man picked up his axe. He cut the mortar into little pieces and threw them in the fire.

When the kind old man came to get his mortar, nothing was left but ashes. He filled a basket with the ashes and sadly carried it home.

"We should leave the ashes on Shiro's grave, dear," said his wife.

　親切なおじいさんはおばあさんに賛成です。ところがおじいさんが外に出たときに、突然風が舞いました。そして灰を果物のなる木へと吹きとばしたのです。すると何がおこったと思います？

　それは真冬のことでした。木々はみんな枯れて枝だけになっています。そこに灰が降りかかると、なんといきなり木々は花でいっぱいです。

　「灰が花に様がわり」おばあさんはびっくりです。

　「これもシロの贈りもの」おじいさんも笑っています。

　おじいさんはとてもうれしくなって、少しばかり踊ります。籠を持って村に出て、灰を宙にまきながら歩いてゆきました。すると、スモモの木、桃の木、そして桜の木と、どれもが皆花ざかり。

　「私は花咲かじじい」おじいさんは叫びます。「枯れ木に花を咲かせましょう！」

　ちょうどそのとき、大殿さまが村を通りかかりました。大殿さまとその配下の人たちは長い旅をおえて、馬に乗ってお城に帰るところでした。

The kind old man agreed. But when he stepped outside, a sudden wind came along. It blew some of the ashes on to the fruit trees. And what do you think happened next?

It was the middle of winter, and all the trees were dead and bare. But when the ashes landed on them, the trees were suddenly covered with flowers.

"The ashes turned to blossoms!" cried the kind old woman.

"It's another present from Shiro!" the old man laughed.

He was so happy that he did a little dance. Then he carried the basket out into the village. As he walked along, he threw ashes into the air. Plum trees, peach trees, and cherry trees flowered behind him.

"I'm Grandfather Flowers!" he cried. "My ashes turn to blossoms!"

Now, just at that time, a great lord happened to be passing through the village. He and his men were riding their horses back to

　「どうしたというのじゃ」大殿さまは、親切なお
じいさんにききました。「何故そちは花咲かじじい
と申しているのじゃ」
　「大殿さまに喜んでお見せ申しあげます」
　親切なおじいさんは、枯れた桜の木にのぼり、
少し灰を撒きました。すると木はたちまち花でい
っぱい。

the castle after a long trip.

"What is the meaning of this?" his lordship asked the kind old man. "Why do you call yourself Grandfather Flowers?"

"I'll gladly show you, your lordship."

The kind old man climbed a dead cherry tree. He threw some of the ashes into the air, and suddenly the tree was full of flowers.

　「みごとじゃ！」大殿さまは叫びました。「この年
よりに小判を授けよ」

　ちょうどそのとき、いじわるじいさんが走りよ
り、親切なおじいさんから籠を取りあげると、

　「私めが、木を焼いて、この灰をつくりましたの
じゃ！」と大きな声で言いました。「その小判は私
めのものでございます。私めが本当の花咲かじじ
いにございます。ご覧あれ」

　いじわるじいさんは枯れた桃の木にのぼって、
残った灰をみんな撒きちらしました。ところが風
が突然吹いたかと思うと、灰はまさに大殿さまの
顔にかかります。

　大殿さまはとても怒りました。

　「この馬鹿ものを鎖につなげ！」大殿さまはそう
命令します。

　いじわるじいさんは、お城につれていかれ、牢
屋にいれられ、そこに長いあいだ閉じこめられて
いたということです。

"Wonderful!" cried his lordship. "Give this old man a bag of gold coins!"

Just then, the mean old man ran up. He took the basket from his neighbor.

"I burned the wood to make these ashes!" he shouted. "That gold belongs to me! I'm the real Grandfather Flowers! Just watch!"

The mean old man ran to a dead peach tree and threw all the ashes into the air. But a sudden wind came along and blew the ashes right in his lordship's face!

His lordship was very angry.

"Put this fool in chains!" he told his men.

They took the mean old man back to the castle and locked him in jail. And that's where he stayed for a very long time.

A Straw Millionaire

わらしべ長者

　昔々、ある村に一人の男が住んでいました。男はとてもいい人ですが、どうも運がありません。男は昼も夜も一生懸命働きますが、いつも貧しく不運なのです。

　ある日、男は観音さまにお参りに行きました。神さまどうか幸せになれますように。男は一日じゅう、飲まず食わずで、お祈りをしました。

　日が暮れて、あたりが暗くなってきたとき、観音さまが現れて申されます。「お前はここを離れるときに転んで、何かを見つけるであろう。お前はそれを手にして、西に行くがよい」

　男がそこを立ちさるとき、転んで何かを見つけます。それは藁（わら）でした。それは何の役にもたたないものですが、男はそれを持って西へと向かいます。

　あぶが一匹飛んできます。男はそれを捕まえると、藁に結びつけ、再び歩きだしました。

Long, long ago there was man living in a village. He was a good man, but he always had bad luck. He worked and worked from morning to night, but he was always poor and unlucky.

One day he prayed to *Kannon*, the Goddess of Mercy, for a happy future. He prayed all day, eating and drinking nothing at all.

When it became dark in the evening, Kannon appeared to him and said, "You are going to fall down and find something when you leave this place. You should take it with you and go west."

When he left the place, he fell down and found something. It was a straw. He thought it was useless, but he picked it up and carried it as he walked toward the west.

A horsefly flew to him. He caught it and tied it on the straw and started walking again.

　町にやってくると、赤ちゃんが藁に結ばれたあぶを見て泣きやみました。そのかわいい赤ちゃんに、男はその藁をあげました。お母さんはお礼にみかんを三つくださいました。

　男はみかんを持って、再び西へ歩きます。すると、道ばたに、若い女の人がいるではありませんか。女の人は喉がかわいていました。そこで男はみかんをあげると、やがて女の人は元気になります。お礼にと、女の人はきれいな絹の織物をくれたのです。
　男はきれいな絹の織物を持って、また西へと歩きます。男はおさむらいさんと、病気の馬に出会

When he arrived in a town, a baby stopped crying when it saw the horsefly on top of the straw. Seeing the happy baby, the man gave the straw to it. The mother thanked him and gave him three oranges.

He started walking west again, carrying the three oranges. He saw a young lady by the side of the road. She wanted water, so he gave her the oranges. Soon she felt better. To thank him, she gave him some beautiful silk cloth.

He started walking west again with the beautiful silk cloth. He met a samurai and

いました。おさむらいは、きれいな織物を見ると、それと馬を交換してくれと頼みました。そしておさむらいは織物を持って東へと立ちさりました。男は病気の馬を一晩じゅう看病しました。すると、その翌朝には馬は元気になったのです。

男は再び馬をつれて西へと歩きます。お城のある町に着いたとき、お金持ちがその馬を見てとても気に入りました。男はお金持ちの家に招かれると、お金持ちの娘がお茶を持ってやってきます。驚いたことに、それはあのみかんを与えた娘だったのです。お金持ちは、この不思議な巡りあわせと、男のありがたい親切に、心を動かされます。そして、娘をこの男に嫁がせようと決心したのでした。

男は、藁から富を手にいれました。観音さまの言うとおり。以来男はずっと、たとえ一本の藁でも大切にします。村の人は男のことをわらしべ長者と呼ぶようになったのでした。

his sick horse. The samurai saw the beautiful cloth and ordered him to give it to him for the horse. The samurai took the cloth and went east. The man looked after the sick horse all night. The horse got well the next morning.

He started walking west again with the horse. When he arrived in a castle town, a rich man saw the horse and liked it very much. The man was invited to the rich man's house, where his daughter brought two cups of tea to them. To his surprise, it was the young lady that he had given the oranges to. The rich man was so moved at the strange meeting and at how kind the man was that he decided his daughter should marry the young man.

The young man became rich from the straw, as Kannon told him. He never forgot to take care of even one piece of straw for the rest of life. He was called *Wara Choja* (the straw millionaire) by the people in the village.

The Fire Boy

火男

　昔々、ある村に、おじいさんとおばあさんが住んでいました。

　やさしいおじいさんはせっせと働き、いつも山に薪をとりに行っていました。ところが、おばあさんはどん欲で、決して働かず、毎日家にいて何もしませんでした。

　ある日のこと、おじいさんが山で薪を探していると、どこかから声が聞こえてきました。「薪をください」

　おじいさんは声のするほうに行ってみました。その声は地面にあいた穴から聞こえてきます。穴の手前に薪を置いてみると、薪は穴の中にどんどん吸い込まれていきます。おじいさんが穴をのぞき込むと、おじいさんも穴に吸い込まれてしまいました。

　そこでは火が燃えていました。おじいさんは火をまつる神社に招かれ、火の神さまと対面しまし

Long, long ago there lived an old man and his wife in a village.

The old man was kind and worked very hard. He always went to the mountain to find wood. But the old woman was greedy and never worked. She did nothing and stayed at home every day.

One day, when he was looking for wood in the mountains, the old man heard a voice from somewhere. It said, "Give me some wood."

The old man went toward the voice. It was coming from a hole in the ground. Whenever he put some wood in front of the hole, it was taken down into it. The moment he looked into it, he was taken down into the hole, too.

There was a fire burning there, and he was invited to a fire shrine. He met the god of fire.

た。神さまはおじいさんに言いました。「薪をくれてありがとう。お礼にこの箱をあげましょう」

　家に帰って箱を開けると、中にはおもしろい顔をした小さな男の子が入っていました。おばあさんはこの贈り物にたいそう腹を立てましたが、やさしいおじいさんは男の子に火男と名づけ、たいせつに育てました。

　男の子は毎日何もせず、すわって自分のへそをこすってばかりいました。おじいさんはへそをさわるなと言いましたが、男の子はやめようとしません。そのうち、へそはだんだん大きくなっていきました。

　おばあさんはまったく気にかけませんでしたが、おじいさんは男の子をかわいそうに思い、男の子のへそをキセルでたたきました。すると、へそから小判が一枚出てきました。もう一度たたくともう一枚。おばあさんは大喜び。それから、おじいさんは一日に三回男の子のへそをそっとたたくようになりました。

　まもなく二人は大金持ちになりましたが、おじいさんはそれでも毎日山に薪をとりに行きました。

The god said to him, "Thank you for your wood. I will give you this box in return for it."

Returning to his house, he found a little boy with a funny face in the box. The old woman was very angry about the present, but the kind old man named the little boy *Hi-Otoko* (Fire Man) and took good care of him.

The little boy did nothing but sit and rub his navel every day. The old man told him not to touch it, but the boy never stopped, and it got very, very big.

The old woman did not care about the boy, but the old man felt sorry for him, so he hit the boy on the navel with his tobacco pipe. A gold coin came out of it. He hit it once more. Another gold coin came out. The old woman was very happy. After that the old man hit the boy lightly on the navel three times a day.

They soon became very rich, but the old man went to the mountain to look for wood every day.

　ある日のこと、やさしいおじいさんが山で働いている間に、おばあさんは大きなキセルを手に持ち、男の子を追いかけて言いました。「このキセルでお前のへそを強くたたけば、お金がたくさん出てくるぞ」

　男の子は逃げ回り、台所で燃えている火の中に飛び込みました。火の神さまがいる火の国に帰ったのです。

　おじいさんは男の子がいなくなったことを嘆き悲しみ、男の子によく似たお面を作り、かまどの近くに置きました。

　日本では、かまどの近くに火男のお面を置く習慣があります。火男という名前が「ひょっとこ」(おもしろい顔)になることもあります。

One day while the kind old man was working in the mountains, the old woman ran after the boy with a big tobacco pipe, saying, "If I hit you hard on the navel with this tobacco pipe, I can get a lot of money."

The little boy ran away from her and jumped into a burning fire in the kitchen. He returned to the country of fire, the place of the fire god.

The old man missed the little boy very much and made a mask that looked like him. He put it near the kitchen stove.

In Japan, there is now a custom that people put a Hi-Otoko mask near a kitchen stove. Sometimes the name is changed to *Hyottoko* (Funny Face).

The God of Poverty

貧乏神

　昔々、ある村に、一組の夫婦が住んでいました。夫婦はいつもせっせと働いていましたが、生活はずっと貧しいままでした。

　「貧乏でいるのが嫌になってきたな。わしらはなんでずっと貧乏なんじゃろう。酒も飲みたいし、お前にきれいな着物も買ってやりたいし、たまには町にも出たいのじゃが」夫が妻にそう言うと、

　「そんなことを考えてもどうしようもないでしょう。畑でせっせと働くのがいちばん良い暮らしですよ」と妻は夫に言いました。

　「それもそうじゃな」夫は答えました。

　夫婦は金持ちではありませんでしたが、村でいちばんの働き者でした。夫は朝から晩まで畑で働き、妻はわらで編んだくつやかごなどを作っていました。

　ある年の大みそか、夫婦はかまどの火のそばで話をしていました。「神さま、ありがとうございま

Long, long ago a husband and his wife were living in a village. They always worked very hard, but their lives were always poor.

"I am tired of being poor. Why are we always so poor? I would like to drink, buy you a beautiful kimono, and go to the town once in a while," said the husband to his wife.

"It is no use thinking about such things. The best way to live is to work hard in our fields," said the wife to her husband.

"Maybe you are right," said the man.

They were not rich, but they were the hardest workers in the village. The man worked in the field from morning to night, while the woman made boots, baskets of straw and so on.

On the last day of a year, they were talking by the cooking fire. "Thank you, God. We

す。私たちはお金を少し蓄えて、新年のおもちを作りました」妻は言いました。

　すると、天井裏からだれかの泣き声が聞こえてきました。貧乏神でした。「そうか。わしらが貧乏なのはお前のせいだったのじゃな。ところで、お前はなぜ泣いているのだ」夫は貧乏神に言いました。

　「今年あなたたちが一生懸命働いたので、私はもうこの家にはいられないのです。もうすぐ福の神がこの家にやってきて、私の代わりを務めます。私は出て行かねばなりません」貧乏神は言いました。

　「では、ここにいられるようにその神を追い出したらどうじゃ」と夫が尋ねると、

　「おなかがぺこぺこで、そんな元気なぞありません」と貧乏神は言いました。

　「あきらめてはいけません！　おもちと魚を好きなだけ食べなさい」妻は言いました。

　「こんなにおいしいごちそうは今まで食べたことがありません。おもちをもう一つください」貧乏神は言いました。

　貧乏神は生まれて初めてたらふく食べました。

saved a little money and made rice cakes for the new year," said the woman.

Then they heard someone crying in the attic of the house. It was the god of poverty. "I see. It was because of you that we are so poor. By the way, why are you crying?" said the husband to the god of poverty.

The god said, "You worked so hard this year that I can not stay in this house. Soon the god of fortune will come to this house to take my place. I must leave here."

"Why don't you make him go away so you can stay here?" asked the husband.

The god said, "I am so hungry that I do not have any energy to do it."

"Don't give up! You can have as many rice cakes and as much fish as you want," said the wife.

The god said, "I have never eaten such a delicious meal before. Give me another rice cake."

He ate and ate for the first time in his life.

たくさん食べて強くなったので、福の神などもう
こわくはありません。貧乏神は相撲取りのように
四股を踏みました。

　福の神は夫婦の家に向かって道を歩いていまし
た。「ああ、今日からここに住むことになるんだな」
と言って、戸をたたきました。「私は福の神です。
今日からここに住み、お金をたくさんあげますよ。
貧乏神め。ここはもうお前の家ではない。すぐに
出て行け！」福の神は言いました。

　「いいえ、私はこの家を出て行きません。ここに
います。おじいさんとおばあさんがあなたを追い
出せと言いました」貧乏神は言いました。
　「貧乏は決して福に負けません」夫婦は言いまし
た。
　「なんだって！　そんなばかな！　なんでそいつの
味方をするんだ。そいつは貧乏神ですよ」もう一人
の神はそう言って家に入ろうとしました。
　貧乏神は福の神に襲いかかり、外に投げ出しま
した。

He had so much that he became strong, and he was no longer afraid of the god of fortune. He stamped his feet on the floor like a sumo wrestler.

The god of fortune was now walking along the street to the house. He said, "Oh, that is the house I will start living in from today," and he knocked on the door, saying, "I am the god of fortune. I am going to live here from now and give you a lot of money. God of poverty, it is no longer your house. Get out at once!"

The god of poverty said, "No, I will never leave this house. I will stay here. The old man and his wife told me to keep you out."

"Poverty will never be defeated by fortune," said the couple.

"What! It is not possible. Why do you cheer for him? He is the god of poverty," said the other god, trying to enter the door.

The god of poverty attacked the god of fortune and threw him out into the street.

「もうこの家には戻ってこないぞ」福の神はそう
言って出て行きましたが、魔法の小槌を忘れてい
きました。

「あいつは何か落としていったぞ。ああ、これは
魔法の小槌だ。小槌がなければ、もうあいつは福
の神ではない。それをもっている私こそが福の神
だ」貧乏神は小槌を拾い上げて夫婦に言いました。
「これは福をもたらす魔法の小槌です。何がほしい
ですか」

夫婦は顔を見合わせました。夫婦が望むものは
何俵かのお米ときれいな着物とわずかなお金でし
た。

「私はもう貧乏神ではありません。福の神です」
神はそう言って天井裏に戻りました。

その後夫婦はせっせと働き、幸せに暮らしまし
た。もう貧乏になることはありませんでした。

"I will never come back to this house," said the god of fortune. The god of fortune went away, but he forgot his magic hammer.

"He dropped something. Oh, it is a magic hammer. Now he has no hammer. He is not the god of fortune now. I have it, so I am the god of fortune," said the god of poverty to the couple, picking it up. "This is a magic hammer which brings you fortune. What do you want?" he said.

They looked at each other. They wanted some straw bags of rice, a beautiful kimono and a little money.

"I am not the god of poverty now. I am the god of fortune," said the god and returned to the attic.

The couple worked very hard after that and had a happy life. They were never poor again.

Six Little Statues

笠地蔵

　昔々、貧しいおじいさんとおばあさんが山に住んでいました。ある年の大みそかのこと、おじいさんが町に薪を売りに行く途中、六人の小さなお地蔵さまを見かけました。

　お地蔵さまは雪をかぶり、いかにも寒そうな様子。おじいさんは雪を払い、言いました。「お地蔵さま。笠もなくて寒かろうな。町で笠を買ってきてあげよう」

　おじいさんは町へ行き、薪を売ってお金を少し稼ぎ、必要なものを買いました。笠を六つ買いたかったのですが、五つしか買えませんでした。

　家に帰る途中、おじいさんは五人のお地蔵さまに笠をかぶせ、最後のお地蔵さまには自分のずきんをかぶせてあげました。
　おじいさんがおばあさんにこの話をすると、おばあさんはニコニコして言いました。「それは良いこ

Long, long ago a poor old man and his wife lived in the mountains. On the last day of the year, the old man went to town to sell some firewood. On his way he saw six little statues called *jizos*.

There was a lot of snow on them, and they looked cold. He cleaned the snow off and said, "You don't even have straw hats. Maybe you feel really cold. I will buy you hats in the town."

He went to the town and got a little money by selling firewood. He bought some things he needed, and he wanted to buy six straw hats, but he was able to buy only five.

On the way home, he put the hats on the heads of five statues, and on the last he put his own hood.

When he told his wife the story, she said happily, "You did a wonderful thing." Then

とをしましたね」そして、二人は寝床につきました。

　その日の真夜中、誰かが歌いながら家に近づいてくる声が聞こえてきました。「やさしいおじいさんのおうちはどこですか。五つの笠と一つのずきんをありがとう。やさしいおじいさんのおうちはどこですか」

　戸口で大きな音がしたので、おじいさんはふとんから出て戸口へと行きました。

　戸を開けると、そこには六俵のお米がありました。おじいさんとおばあさんは幸せな新年を迎えることができました。

they went to bed.

At midnight they heard someone coming to their house, singing, "Where is the house of the kind old man? We are glad to have five straw hats and a hood. Where is the kind old man's house?"

Hearing a loud sound at the door, he got out of his bed and went to the door.

Opening the door, he found six big straw bags of rice there. The old man and his wife had a happy New Year.

Urashima Taro

浦島太郎

浦島太郎

　昔々、あるところに浦島太郎という心やさしい
漁師が住んでいました。ある日、海辺を歩いてい
ると、浦島太郎は亀に出会います。村の子どもた
ちがいじめていたのを助けてあげたのです。

　数日の後、浦島太郎はいつものように、漁に出
かけました。すると、あのとき助けた亀が、浦島
太郎のところにやってくるではありませんか。
　「あのとき助けていただいた亀でございます。お
姫さまが、竜宮城でお礼のおもてなしをしたいと
申しております」亀はそう言いました。

　亀は、浦島太郎を甲羅のうえに乗せると、海に
もぐって竜宮城につれていきました。
　竜宮城は、珊瑚がいっぱいの素晴らしいところ
でした。たくさんの魚がまわりを泳いでいます。
しかも、浦島太郎は、乙姫さまというきれいなお
姫さまに出会います。こんな美しい人ははじめて
です。

Long, long ago there lived a kind fisherman called Urashima Taro. One day, while walking along the beach, he saw a turtle. The village children were doing mean things to the turtle, but he saved it.

Several days later, he was fishing as always when the turtle he had helped came to him from the sea.

"I am the turtle that you saved the other day. A princess told me to bring you to the *Ryugujo* (Dragon Palace) to thank you," said the turtle.

It took him on its back to the Ryugujo under the sea.

The Ryugujo was a wonderful place filled with beautiful coral, and there were many fish swimming around in it. Even better, he met a beautiful princess named Otohime. He had never seen such a beautiful lady before.

「浦島太郎さん。いつまでも、こころゆくまでおくつろぎください」乙姫さまはそう言いました。

浦島太郎は、時の経つのも忘れ、夢のような日々を送ります。しかし、何年かして、浦島太郎は昔住んでいた村と、年老いた母親のことを思いだします。そろそろ帰らなければ。乙姫さまは、お別れに小さな箱をくださいました。そして言いました。

"Mr. Urashima, please enjoy yourself here as long as you wish," said the princess.

He forgot the passing of time. Life there was like a dream. But after several years he remembered his old village and his old mother. It was time to go home. When she said goodbye to him, the princess gave him a little box as a present.

　「浦島太郎さん。これは玉手箱という魔法の箱。何か困ったことがあったとき、それを開けてくださいね」

　浦島太郎が亀の背に乗って村に帰ると、住んでいた家もなく、年老いた母もいません。村はとても変わってしまっていたのです。

　浦島太郎はどうしていいやらわかりません。そこで、あの小さな箱を開けたのです。すると煙が出てきて、浦島太郎は、瞬くまに、長く白いひげをはやしたおじいさんに変わってしまいました。

　海のしたで楽しく過ごしていたあいだに、この世では何百年も経っていたのです。浦島太郎は、いま自分がどこにいるのやら、これが夢かどうかすらわからなくなったということです。

She said, "Mr. Urashima, this is a magic box called a *tamate-bako*. When you are in trouble, you can open it."

When he went back home on the turtle, he could not find his house or his old mother, and he found his village had changed a lot.

He did not know what to do. At last he opened the little box. When he opened it, white smoke came out of it, and he suddenly became an old man with a long white beard.

While he was having a happy time under the sea, hundreds of years had passed on Earth. He was not sure where he was now and did not know if it was a dream or not.

Issun Boshi

一寸法師

　昔々、なにわに若い夫婦が住んでいました。二人はいつも仲がよく、皆から好かれていました。でも、二人には子どもがいません。そこである日、二人は住吉神社にお参りに行きました。

　「どうか子どもを授けたまえ」二人は神さまにそうお祈りをしました。「どんなに小さな子どもでも構いません、一人子どもを授けたまえ」
　するとどうでしょう。数ヵ月ほどして、妻が小さな男の子を生んだのです。それはとても小さな子どもでした。指ほどの大きさもありません。でもとても元気で生き生きとしていました。二人は心からその子を大切にし、一寸法師と名づけたのでした。

　一寸法師とは、小さい子どもという意味です。やがて一寸法師は5歳になりました。でも一寸法師の身長は変わりません。7歳になっても、10歳になっても、そして12歳になっても。

Long, long ago in Naniwa, there lived a young man and his wife. They were both good people, and they loved each other very much. But, sadly, they had no children. One day they went to Sumiyoshi Shrine to pray.

"Won't you send us a child?" they asked the god of the shrine. "Just one little child of our own, no matter how small!"

And what do you think happened? Some months later, the lady gave birth to a little baby boy. A very little one, in fact. This baby was no bigger than your finger. But he was healthy and full of life, and his parents loved him with all their hearts. They named him Issun Boshi.

Issun Boshi means "Little One Inch." By the time he reached the age of five, Issun Boshi was still only an inch tall. The same was true at seven, and even at ten and twelve.

　他の子と違うことは、子どもにとっては大変です。でも、他の子がチビだといって笑うと、一寸法師も一緒になって笑うのです。一寸法師は誰にでもいつもやさしく、にこにこしています。そう、一寸法師の心はとても大きかったのです。

＊

　一寸法師は大きな夢を持っていました。ある日のこと、一寸法師はお父さんとお母さんのところに行って、深く頭をさげました。

　「父上、母上。私はこれから都に行きたいと思います」一寸法師はそう言いました。

　「京に行くとな。一人でかい」お母さんはそうたずねました。

　「はい。そこは日本で最もすばらしいところだと聞いています。そこで運を試してみたいのです」一寸法師はそう答えました。

　「しかし、お前はまだ子どもじゃないか」

　二人はかわいい我が子に旅に出てほしくはありません。しかし、とうとう二人は一寸法師に説得されてしまいました。

　「わかったぞ。息子よ」お父さんは言いました。「私たちは、お前には自分の望みをあきらめないよ

It wasn't easy being so different from other children. But when the others laughed at his size, Issun Boshi only laughed along with them. He was kind to all and always smiling. In other words, he had a very big heart.

*

He also had big dreams. One day, Issun Boshi went to his parents and bowed deeply.

"Mother, Father," he said, "I want to go to the capital."

"To the City of Kyo?" said his mother. "All by yourself?"

"Yes," said Issun Boshi. "They say it's the most wonderful place in all Japan. I want to try my luck there."

"But you're so young…"

His parents didn't want their dear boy to go, but at last they agreed.

"Very well, son," his father said. "We always taught you to follow your heart. Go to

うにと教えてきた。都に行って、立派な人になり
なさい」

　「ありがとうございます。父上」

　一寸法師はすぐに旅じたくを整えます。お母さ
んは、大切にしていた縫い針を刀として一寸法師
にわたすと、藁を帯に結びつけて、刀の鞘にして
あげました。そしてお父さんは、一寸法師のため
にお椀を持ってきて、舟にして、お箸でお椀の舟
を漕いでゆくようにしてあげました。

　次の日の朝、皆で川まで歩いてゆくと、一寸法
師はお椀の舟によじのぼり、それに乗ると、お箸
で陸を押して川に出てゆきます。お父さんとお母
さんは、手を振って別れを惜しむのでした。

　「気をつけるんだよ。自分を信じてな！」

　「母上、父上、おさらばです。必ず立派な人にな
って参ります」

　少しずつ、くる日もくる日も一寸法師はお椀の
舟をあやつって川をのぼってゆきました。時には
強い風や大雨で、何度もお椀の舟はひっくりかえ
りそうになりました。そして何度も鳥や魚と闘わ

the capital and become a great man."

"Thank you, Father!"

Issun Boshi was soon ready for his trip. His mother gave him her finest sewing needle to use as a sword, and she tied a straw to his belt to carry the sword in. His father gave him a soup bowl to use as a boat and a chopstick to use as an oar.

The next morning, they all walked down to the river together. Issun Boshi climbed into the soup bowl and pushed off with his chopstick. His mother and father waved goodbye.

"Good luck, son! Never stop believing in yourself!"

"Goodbye, Mother! Goodbye, Father! I'll become a great man, I promise!"

Little by little, day after day, Issun Boshi pushed his soup bowl boat up the river. He met with strong winds and hard rains. More than once his little boat almost turned over.

なければなりませんでした。でも、一寸法師はあ
きらめませんでした。

　そしてついに京についたとき、一寸法師は夢を
見ているようでした。きれいな通りには人や馬や
手押し車がたくさん。そして店々ではこの世にあ
るものはなんでも売っています。

And more than once he had to fight off birds and fish. But he never gave up.

When at last he reached the City of Kyo, he thought he must be dreaming. The beautiful streets were filled with people and horses and carts, and the shops sold everything under the sun.

「日本一の町だ」一寸法師は思いました。「皆が言っていたようにすごい町だ」

一寸法師は五条通りから三条通りへと歩いてゆきます。そこには、大きな家の門がありました。

「これはとても偉い人の家に違いない。ここで働けるか聞いてみよう」一寸法師は思いました。

一寸法師は、門からまっすぐ大きな玄関へと歩いてゆくと、そのすぐ前に立ち、大きな声で

「ごめんください！」と言いました。

三条の君はちょうど家にいたので、子どもの大きな声を聞いて玄関を開けましたが、そこには誰もおりません。

「こちらです」一寸法師は叫びました。

なんと小さな子どもでしょう。三条の君はびっくり仰天。

「おまえは誰かえ」

「私はなにわの一寸法師と申します。立派な人に

"The greatest city in Japan!" he thought. "It's just as wonderful as people say!"

He walked from Gojo, the fifth block, to Sanjo, the third. And there he came to the gate of a great big house.

"This must be the home of a very important man," he thought. "I'll ask if I can work for him!"

Issun Boshi marched right through the gate and all the way up to the big front entrance. He stood on the step and called out at the top of his voice:

"Excuse me!"

The Lord of Sanjo happened to be just inside the entrance. He heard the boy's shout and opened the door himself. But he couldn't see anyone.

"Down here, sir!" cried Issun Boshi.

Lord Sanjo was surprised to see such a small person.

"Who are you?" he said.

"I am Issun Boshi of Naniwa. I want to

なりたいんです。お殿さまにお仕えできますでしょうか」

　三条の君は笑いだしました。とても面白そうな子に思えたのです。

　「お前のような者をやとうとは。望むところじゃ」

　一寸法師はすぐにこのお偉い方の一家の一員として迎えられました。しっかり働き、勉強し、いつも与えられた仕事は精いっぱいがんばりました。一寸法師は皆から好かれています。三条の君の娘でとてもきれいなお姫さまはとくに一寸法師を気にいっていました。一寸法師はこの世で一番かわいいと、お姫さまは思い、二人はすぐによい友だちになりました。

＊

　夏が過ぎ、秋が来たかと思えば、もう冬です。そして春のある日、お姫さまは清水寺に桜を見にいきたいと言いました。若い男たちや女たちが一緒にお姫さまと花見に行きます。一寸法師も一緒でした。

　お寺に向かって森を歩いてゆくと、藪のなかで

become a great man. May I work for you?"

Lord Sanjo laughed. He found this young man very interesting.

"I can use a man like you, Issun Boshi," he said. "Welcome!"

Issun Boshi soon became like a member of the great man's family. He worked and studied hard and always did his best at every job. Everyone liked him—especially Lord Sanjo's beautiful daughter, Ohime-sama. She thought Issun Boshi was the cutest thing in the world, and they soon became the best of friends.

*

Summer passed, and then autumn and winter. One day in spring, Ohime-sama said she wanted to see the cherry blossoms at Kiyomizu Temple. A group of young men and women agreed to go with her, and Issun Boshi joined them.

They were all walking through the forest

音がします。突然大きな青鬼が一行のまえに立ちはだかりました。鬼は馬ほど大きく、目は真っ赤、そして歯は長く尖っています。けたたましい音を出しながら、お姫さまのところにやってくるではありませんか。お姫さまは気を失って倒れてしまいました。

　他の男も女も皆一目散に逃げてゆきます。でも一寸法師だけは畏^{おそ}れませんでした。一寸法師は鬼とお姫さまのあいだに立って、あの針の刀を引きぬきます。

　「こちらは三条の君のお姫さまであるぞ。すぐに立ちされ、さもなければお前を打ちのめしてやる」

　鬼は笑いました。
　「なんだと。お前は朝飯のおかずにもならぬなあ！」鬼はそう言うと二本の指で一寸法師をつまみあげました。そして、高く持ちあげたかと思うと、自分の口の中に放りこみます。

　気がつくと、一寸法師は、長くて暗いトンネル

on the way to the temple, when they heard a noise in the brush. Suddenly a big blue demon jumped out in front of them. This demon was the size of a horse and had red eyes and long, pointed teeth. It made a terrible noise and reached for Ohime-sama. She fell to the ground in a faint.

The other young men and women all turned and ran away at once. Issun Boshi alone was not afraid. He stood his ground, between the demon and Ohime-sama, and pulled out his needle sword.

"This lady is the daughter of Lord Sanjo!" he shouted. "Leave her alone, or I'll cut you down!"

The demon laughed.

"Why, you're not even big enough to make a good breakfast!" it said. It reached down and caught Issun Boshi between two fingers. Then it lifted him high in the air and dropped him into its mouth.

Issun Boshi found himself in a long, dark

のなかにいます。でも一寸法師はひるみません。刀の切っ先を、トンネルのやわらかい壁に突きさします。そしてそれを抜くとまた突きさします。

　「俺さまのなかで、これは痛い！」鬼は叫んでころがりまわります。「やめろ！　降参だ！」

＊

　一寸法師は、鬼の口から飛びでると、鬼の足に針を突きたてました。鬼は泣きながら一目散に逃げてゆきます。

　お姫さまはそのときすでに気がついていました。

　「私はすべてを見ていました。私の命の恩人ね」お姫さまはいとおしそうに一寸法師を見つめています。

　「とんでもございません」一寸法師は言いました。

　「あなたはすてきな方。おや、見てごらんなさい」

　お姫さまはそう言うと、地面にころがった奇妙な木づちを指さしました。

　「これはなんでしょう」一寸法師が不思議に思うと、

　「鬼が残した魔法の木づちですよ」とお姫さまが言うのです。「あなたの望みはなんでもかなえられるのです！　おっしゃってください。私の大事な人」

tunnel. But even now he wasn't afraid. He pushed the point of his sword into the soft wall of the tunnel. Then he pulled it out, and then he pushed it back in.

"My insides! They hurt!" the demon shouted and danced about. "Stop! You win!"

*

Issun Boshi jumped back out of the demon's mouth and drove his needle into its foot. The demon cried and ran for its life.

Ohime-sama was awake now.

"I saw everything!" she said and looked at Issun Boshi with the light of love in her eyes. "My hero!"

"Oh, it was nothing," he said.

"You were wonderful!" she said. "But look!"

She pointed at a strange hammer on the ground.

"What is it?" said Issun Boshi.

"The demon dropped his magic hammer!" she said. "Any wish you make with this will come true! What do you wish for, my hero?"

　一寸法師は、木づちに手をおくと目を閉じました。そして目を開けると、一寸法師は大きくなっていたのです。

　お姫さまは口を大きく開けてびっくり仰天。
　「一寸法師。あなたはとても背が高くてすてきな人」
　一寸法師の名は都に知れわたり、都で出世します。そしてお姫さまと結ばれて、大きな家に二人で越してゆきました。やがて二人はなにわに行って、一寸法師のお父さんとお母さんを都につれてもどりました。
　そして幾ひさしく幸せに暮らしましたとさ。

Issun Boshi put his hand on the hammer and closed his eyes. When he opened them again, he was fully grown.

Ohime-sama's mouth fell open.

"Oh, Issun Boshi!," she said. "You're so tall! And so nice looking!"

Soon Issun Boshi was a famous and important man in the capital. He and Ohime-sama married and moved into a big house of their own. In time, they traveled to Naniwa and brought his parents back with them.

And they all lived happily ever after.

Twelve Years of
Animals

十二支

　昔々、十二月の最後の日、神さまは動物たちに言いました。「新年の最初の日である明日、私の家に来なさい。最初に来た十二人に一年ずつあげよう」

　ねこは神さまの家に行く日を聞いていなかったので、ねずみに尋ねました。ねずみはねこに、その日は新年の二日だとおしえました。

　大みそかに、うしは神さまの家をめざして出発しました。うしは歩みが遅く、時間がかかることがわかっていたからです。ねずみはそれを見て、うしの背中に飛び乗りました。
　元日の朝早く、うしは神さまの御殿に着きました。
　門が開くやいなや、ねずみは飛び降り、うしより先に神さまの元へ走りました。
　「ねずみ、お前は一番だ。お前に最初の年をあげよう」神さまは言いました。

Long, long ago, on the last day of December, God said to the animals, "Tomorrow, on the first day of the new year, you should come to visit me. I am going to give one year to each of the first 12 animals that comes to see me."

The cat didn't hear the day when animals should go to visit God, so she asked the mouse. The mouse told her that she should go on the second day of the year.

On the last day of the year, the cow started going to see God because she walked slowly, and she knew it would take her a long time. The mouse saw her and jumped on her back.

The cow reached God's palace early in the morning on the first day of the year.

As soon as the gate opened, the mouse jumped down and ran to God ahead of the cow.

"Mouse, you are the first. I'll give you the first year," said God.

　「うし、お前は二番だ。お前に二番目の年をあげよう」神さまは言いました。

　「とら、お前は三番だ。お前に三番目の年をあげよう」神さまは言いました。

　「うさぎ、お前は四番だ。お前に四番目の年をあげよう」神さまは言いました。

　「たつ、お前は五番だ。お前に五番目の年をあげよう」神さまは言いました。

　「へび、お前は六番だ。お前に六番目の年をあげよう」神さまは言いました。

　「うま、お前は七番だ。お前に七番目の年をあげよう」神さまは言いました。

　「ひつじ、お前は八番だ。お前に八番目の年をあげよう」神さまは言いました。

　「さる、お前は九番だ。お前に九番目の年をあげよう」神さまは言いました。

　「とり、お前は十番だ。お前に十番目の年をあげよう」神さまは言いました。

　「いぬ、お前は十一番だ。お前に十一番目の年をあげよう」神さまは言いました。

　「いのしし、お前は十二番だ。お前に十二番目の年をあげよう」神さまは言いました。

"Cow, you are the second. I'll give you the second year," said God.

"Tiger, you are the third. I'll give you the third year," said God.

"Rabbit, you are the fourth. I'll give you the fourth year," said God.

"Dragon, you are the fifth. I'll give you the fifth year," said God.

"Snake, you are the sixth. I'll give you the sixth year," said God.

"Horse, you are the seventh. I'll give you the seventh year," said God.

"Sheep, you are the eighth. I'll give you the eighth year," said God.

"Monkey, you are the ninth. I'll give you the ninth year," said God.

"Hen, you are the tenth. I'll give you the tenth year," said God.

"Dog, you are the eleventh. I'll give you the eleventh year," said God.

"Boar, you are the twelfth. I'll give you the twelfth year," said God.

　次の日、ねこは神さまの家に行きましたが、行くのが遅すぎました。ねこはねずみにだまされたことを知り、かんかんに怒りました。そういうわけで、ねこは今でもねずみを見かけるたびに、ねずみを追いかけてしとめようとします。

The next day, the cat came to see God, but she was too late. She knew the mouse had fooled her. She got so angry at the mouse that even today she runs after him and tries to kill him every time she sees him.

A Gift from Heaven

天福地福

　昔々、ある村に、やさしいおじいさんとおばあさんが住んでいました。その隣にはたいそう怠け者のおじいさんが住んでいました。

　ある夜、やさしいおじいさんは夢を見て、翌朝おばあさんに夢の話をしました。「いい夢を見たよ。天から福を授かったんじゃ」

　「それはいい夢じゃなあ」とおばあさんは答え、二人はにっこりとほほえみました。

　その後、二人は小さな畑に野良仕事に出かけました。おじいさんが鍬を地面に突っ込むと、なにやら音がして小さな壺が出てきました。「これはなんじゃ？」おじいさんが尋ねると、「さあ、開けてみたらどうかのう」とおばあさんは言いました。

　おじいさんが壺を開けてみると、驚いたことに、小判がいっぱい入っているではありませんか。おじいさんとおばあさんはびっくり仰天。しばらく口もきけず身動きもできず。

　怠け者のおじいさんは、木の陰からこの様子を

Long, long ago, there lived a kind old man and his wife in a village. Next to them lived another old man, who was very lazy.

One night, the good old man had a dream and told his wife about it in the morning. He said, "I had a good dream. I was given a gift from Heaven."

"That's a good dream," said his wife. Both of them smiled.

Later, they went to their small field to work. The old man heard a sound when he put his hoe in the ground. He found a small pot. "What's this?" he asked his wife. She said, "I have no idea. Why don't you open it?"

The man opened it, and to his surprise, he found a lot of money in it. He and his wife were so surprised that they couldn't speak or move for a few minutes.

The lazy old man was watching them from

じっと見ていて、「なんじゃと？　小判いっぱいの壺じゃと？」と独り言を言いました。

　「これは夢に出てきた天からの福かのう？」おばあさんが尋ねると、「いや。夢では天から福を授かるという話じゃった。これは地からやってきたから、天からではなく地からの福じゃ」とおじいさんは言いました。「それでは、地に返しましょうか」とおばあさんが言い、二人は壺を土の中に戻しました。

　「なんてばかなやつらだ！　小判はわしのものだ」怠け者のおじいさんは言いました。

　その日の夜のこと、怠け者のおじいさんはくわをもって畑にやってきました。壺を掘り出して開けてみると、蛇がにょろにょろにょろにょろ出てきます。怠け者のおじいさんはいそいで壺にふたをして、その壺をもってやさしいおじいさんの家に走って行きました。「わしにうそをついたな。ひどい目にあわせてやろう」とかんかんに怒っていました。

　屋根の上に登り、天窓から家の中をのぞくと、おじいさんとおばあさんがいろりの前でお茶を飲

behind a tree. "What? A pot full of money?" said the lazy man to himself.

"Is this the gift from Heaven that you saw in the dream?" asked the old woman. The old man said, "No, the dream said that I will get a gift from Heaven. This came from the ground. This is a gift not from Heaven but from the ground." The woman said, "Let's return it to the ground." They put the pot back in the ground.

"What fools! That money is mine," said the lazy old man.

That night, he returned to the field with a hoe. He dug up the pot and opened it, but a lot of snakes came out of it one after another. He quickly put the lid back on the pot and ran with it to the house of the good old man. He was very angry and said, "They lied to me. I'm going to do something terrible to them."

He climbed up on the roof and looked inside the house from the chimney. The old

んでいました。

　「わしにうそをついたな。蛇でもくらえ！」怠け者のおじいさんは壺を開けて蛇を投げ落としましたが、蛇は小判に変わり、おじいさんとおばあさんに天から小判が降りそそぎました。

　「これが夢でお告げのあった天からの福じゃな」おじいさんは言いました。

　おじいさんとおばあさんは、喜びのあまり踊り出しました。

couple were drinking tea by the fire.

"They lied to me. I'll give them snakes," the lazy old man said. He opened the pot and dropped the snakes, but they changed into money when they fell down. Money poured from Heaven onto the old couple.

"This is the gift from Heaven I was promised in my dream," said the old man.

They were so happy they began to dance.

The Golden Boy

金太郎

金太郎

　昔々のこと、足柄山という山に、金太郎という
男の子がお母さんといっしょに住んでいました。
金太郎のお父さんは、おさむらいで京都に住んで
いましたが、戦(いくさ)で死んでしまったのです。

　お母さんは、戦を避けるために、山の奥深くへ
金太郎をつれてゆきました。「どんなことをしてで
も、この子を夫のように立派なさむらいに育てな
ければ」お母さんはそのように自分に言いきかせて
いました。
　二人は洞窟のなかに住んでいたので、誰も見つ
けることができません。食べるものがなかったの
で、お母さんは金太郎のために果物や木の実、野
いちごなどを摘んでいました。
　お母さんは、昔はとてもきれいでした。でも、今では
そんな美貌もすたれてしまっています。お母さんのき
れいな着物も汚れてやぶれてしまいました。二人は貧
しいけど、お母さんは金太郎を大切に思い、いつもた
くさんの食べ物を金太郎のために用意していました。

Long, long ago, on a mountain called Mt. Ashigara, there lived a young boy called *Kintaro* (the Golden Boy) and his mother. His father had been a samurai in Kyoto, but he was killed in a war.

His mother, who ran away from the fighting, brought Kintaro deep into the mountains. "I must make my son a great samurai like my husband any way I can," she said to herself.

The two lived in a cave so no one would find them. She picked fruit, nuts and berries for him because they did not have any other food.

At one time, she had been very beautiful, but now she lost her beauty. Her beautiful clothes became dirty and worn out. They were poor, but she loved Kintaro and gave him a lot of food.

　やがて、金太郎は元気いっぱいの楽しい子ども
に育ちました。毎日、金太郎は山に住む多くの動
物たちと相撲をとって、次から次へと動物たちを
投げとばしていました。

　「くまさん。君の番だ、かかってこい！」金太郎
はそう言うと、金太郎と同じぐらい強い大きなく
まと戦います。長い取りくみののち、金太郎はく
まを投げたのでした。

　相撲のあと、金太郎は動物たちと森に走ってゆ
きました。そして、猿からは木ののぼりかた、鹿
からは森のなかでの走りかたを学びます。

Soon he grew up to be a cheerful boy with a lot of energy. Every day he did sumo with the many animals living on the mountain. He threw one animal after another.

"Dear Bear, it's your turn. Come on!" he said, and fought with the big bear, which was just as strong as he was. After a long match, he threw it.

After the fight, he ran in the forest with the animals. He was taught how to climb trees by a monkey and how to run in the woods by a deer.

友だちの一人に川に住む大きな鯉がいました。金太郎は、その鯉が水からはねて飛びでたとき、助けてあげたのです。金太郎は早瀬のなかを鯉が泳ぐとき、背に乗って遊びます。

雨が降ると、金太郎は一日中動物たちと洞窟にいます。ねずみやりす、狐、あなぐま、猿、うさぎ、くま、それにもっと他の動物たちにも食べものを与えるのです。ですから金太郎は動物たちの人気者です。

そんな金太郎を見て、お母さんは、神さまにお祈りをします。「金太郎はきっと立派なさむらいになります！」

何年かが過ぎて、春がやってきました。ある日金太郎は、動物たちと隣の山に旅に出ました。

金太郎は大きなくまのうえに乗って、まさかりを担いで、猿やりす、そしてむじなに狐、そして猪や鹿をつれてゆきます。皆で楽しく旅をしました。

崖までくると、したに流れの速い川があるではありませんか。

One of his friends was a big carp living in a river. He had saved the fish when it jumped out of the water. He enjoyed riding on the carp as it swam up the fast-moving river.

When it was raining, he spent all day with the animals in a cave. He gave food to mice, squirrels, foxes, badgers, monkeys, rabbits, bears and other animals. He was very popular among them.

Looking at her son, his mother prayed to God, "May he be a great samurai!"

Several years passed, and spring came. One day, he went on a trip to the next mountain with the animals.

He sat on a big bear, carrying his hatchet on his shoulder, and with him were a mouse, a squirrel, a monkey, a rabbit, a raccoon, a fox, a boar and a deer. They really enjoyed the trip.

Reaching a cliff, they found a big river moving fast under them.

「川の流れが速すぎて、わたれないぞ」金太郎は言いました。

「僕が大きな木を押したおして、橋をつくるよ」くまは言いました。でも、木はとてもがっしりしています。

猪が木にむかって走ってきて、頭をぶつけますが、葉っぱが動いただけでした。

「よし、僕がやってみよう」金太郎はそう言うと、木の前に立って何度もそれを押しました。

動物たちはびっくり。木が動いて、ついに大きな音とともに倒れたではありませんか。そしてやっと崖をわたれる橋ができたのです。

みんなとてもうれしくなりました。そのとき、誰かがうしろで話しかけています。「なんと力のある子なのじゃ」そこには一人のさむらいが、配下をつれて立っていました。

「わしの名は源頼光じゃ。わしの家来になってはくれぬか」

「おさむらいになれるのですか」金太郎はびっくりしてそう言いました。

「間違いなく、わしの家来のなかでも最も立派なさむらいになれるじゃろう」

"The river is so fast that we can't cross it," said Kintaro.

"I will push down a big tree and make a bridge," said the bear, but the tree was too strong.

The boar ran at the tree and hit it with his head, but only the leaves moved.

"OK, I will try," said Kintaro, and he stood in front of the tree. He pushed and pushed.

To the animals' surprise, the tree moved and then fell with a big noise, making a bridge between the two cliffs.

Everyone felt very happy. Then somebody spoke to them from behind. The voice said, "What a powerful boy you are!" A samurai and his men were standing there.

"My name is Minamoto-No-Yorimitsu. Why don't you join me?"

"Can I be a samurai?" asked Kintaro with surprise.

"I am sure you'll be one of my greatest samurai," said Yorimitsu.

　金太郎はお母さんのいる洞窟にもどると、「私は父上のような立派なさむらいになって参ります」と言いました。お母さんはうれしくて目に涙を浮かべます。しかし、金太郎と別れることは寂しいかぎりです。

　山を去るとき、動物たちもお母さんも悲しそうに金太郎を見おくりました。

　「今まで仲よくしてくれてありがとう。絶対みんなのことは忘れないよ。そして大好きなお母さん。きっと帰って参りますから」金太郎は何度も手を振りながらそう言いました。

　何年かして、金太郎は立派なおさむらいになって、坂田金時と名のります。京都では、金太郎は頼光の四天王のひとりに数えられ、大江山に住む鬼たちも退治しました。

　金太郎は、お母さんを京都に招き、末ながく幸せに暮らしたということです。

He returned to the cave where his mother lived and said to her, "I will be a great samurai like my father." She was so happy that tears came to her eyes, but she was sad to say goodbye to him.

When he left the mountain, the animals and his mother saw him off with sad faces.

"Thank you for being my friends. I will never forget you. I love you, Mom. I am sure I will return home in the future," said Kintaro, waving his hands again and again.

A few years later he became a great samurai named Sakata-No-Kintoki. In Kyoto, he was chosen as one of the four most important of Yorimitsu's men and killed demons living on a mountain called Mt. Oe.

He invited his mother to Kyoto, and they lived together happily ever after.

The Old are Cleverer than the Young

うば捨て山

　昔々、年寄りが嫌いだというわがままな殿さまがいました。ある日、殿さまは家来に命じて、国中にお触れ書きの看板を立てさせました。お触れ書きにはこう書いてあります。「六十歳以上の年寄りは、山に捨てなければならない。このお触れを破った家族は死罪とする」お触れに従わないと殿さまに命を奪われることになるのが怖くて、みんな、しかたなく従っていました。

　そのころ、その国には、一人の若者が年老いた母親と住んでいました。母親は言いました。「息子よ。かあさんは六十歳になったから、山に連れて行かねばならないよ」息子は悲しそうに言いました。「かあさん、そんな恐ろしいことはできません」母親は息子を見て言いました。「隣のお年寄りたちももう山に連れて行かれたから、お前は心配しなくていいよ」

　ようやく、若者は母親を山に連れて行く決心が

Long, long ago, there was a selfish lord, who didn't like old people. One day, he ordered his men to set up message boards all over the country. The boards said, 'Anyone who is over 60 years old must be taken to the mountains and left to die. Any family that does not do this will be killed.' Everyone had to do it because they were afraid the lord would kill them if they didn't.

At that time, there was a young man who lived with his old mother in the country. The mother said, "My son, I am 60 years old. You have to take me to the mountain." The son was very sad and said, "Mother, I can't do such a terrible thing." His mother looked at him and said, "The old people who live next-door have already been taken to the mountain, so you needn't worry."

Finally, the young man decided he had to

つき、母親をおぶって山を登りました。

　山の頂上まで来たものの、やはり母親を置いて
いくことができず、若者は母親をおぶって、その
夜こっそりと家に帰りました。そして、家の裏に
ある古い納屋に母親を隠しました。

　数日後、殿さまは灰で縄を作れというお触れを
出しました。息子は言いました。「かあさん、殿さ
まが灰で縄を作れというお触れを出したよ。やっ
てみたけど無理だった。これができなければ年貢
をたくさん取られてしまう」

　母親は言いました。「息子よ。それは簡単じゃよ。
おしえてあげよう。まず、わら縄を一本塩水につ
けて、乾いたら焼けばいい」
　若者は言われたとおりに灰縄を作り、殿さまに
持って行きました。殿さまは言いました。「これは
見事じゃ。さて、もっと難しい問題を出そう。こ
の棒を見よ。どちら側が根で、どちら側が枝かわ
かるか」

take his mother to the mountain. He carried her on his back and climbed the mountain.

At the top of the mountain, he decided he could not leave his mother, and he returned home secretly that night with her on his back. He hid his mother in an old barn behind his house.

Several days later, the lord ordered the people to make a rope out of ash. The son said, "Mother, the lord ordered us to make a rope out of ash. We tried it, but it was impossible. If we can't do it, we'll have to pay more taxes to him."

His mother said, "Son, it's easy. I'll teach you. First, take a piece of straw rope, put it into salt water, dry it, and then burn it."

The young man did what he was told and brought the rope made of ash to the lord. The lord said, "That's wonderful. Now I'll give you a more difficult question. Look at this stick. Tell me which end of this is the root and which end is the bough."

　若者は棒を家に持ち帰りました。どうしたらよいかわからず、母親に相談しました。

　母親は言いました。「そんなの簡単じゃよ。水がいっぱい入った壺を持ってきなさい」若者は水を用意してその中に棒を入れました。母親は言いました。「ほら！　水の中にあるほうが根で、水の中にないほうが枝じゃよ」若者は殿さまのところへ行き、答えを言いました。

　殿さまは言いました。「お前は賢いやつじゃ。さて、今度はいちばん難しい問題を出そう。人がたたかなくても鳴る太鼓を作ってみよ」

　若者が帰ってきたとき、顔が青ざめていました。母親に助けを求めると、
　「そんなの簡単じゃよ。山で蜂を何匹か捕まえてくるんじゃ」と母親は言いました。

　母親は蜂を太鼓の中に入れて蓋をしました。すると、太鼓はひとりでに鳴り出しました。

The young man took it back to his house. He didn't know what to do, so he asked his mother for advice.

The mother said, "It's very easy. Bring me a pot full of water." The young man prepared the water and put the stick into it. The mother said, "Look. One end is in the water. That's the root. The other is not in the water. That's the bough." The young man went to the lord to tell him the answer.

The lord said, "You're a clever man. I'm now going to give you the most difficult question. You must make a drum which can make sound without being hit by a man."

When the young man came home, his face was white. He went to his mother for help.

"It's very easy. All you have to do is get a few bees from the mountain," said his mother.

The mother put the bees into the drum and closed it again. The drum began to make a sound by itself.

　若者が殿さまに太鼓を渡すと、殿さまは言いました。「お前は本当に賢いやつじゃ。この三つの難題はすべてお前が自分で解いたのか」

　若者は言いました。「実は、難題を解いたのは私ではありません。私の母です。年寄りを捨てるというお触れが出されましたが、私にはそんな恐ろしいことはできませんでした。母は納屋におります。年寄りは若い者のようには働けませんが、若い者より多くのことを知っております」

　殿さまはしばし考えてから言いました。「そうかもしれぬな。わしが間違っておった」殿さまは家来に命じて、お触れ書きの看板を立てさせました。お触れ書きにはこう書いてありました。「国中の若者は年寄りを大切にすること」

The young man gave the drum to the lord. The lord said, "You're a very clever man. Did you answer the three difficult questions by yourself?"

The young man said, "To tell the truth, it was not I that answered them. It was my mother. You ordered us to throw away the old, but I couldn't do such a terrible thing. She's in my barn. Old people can't work as hard as young people, but they know much more than we do."

The lord thought about it, and finally he said, "You're right, and I was wrong." The lord sent out his men to put up message boards that said young people all over the country should take good care of the old.

Rice Ball
Rolling Down

おむすびころりん

　昔々、ある村におじいさんとおばあさんが住ん
でいました。二人はやさしくて正直で、働き者だ
ったので、みんなから「やさしいおじいさんとおば
あさん」と呼ばれていました。ある日のこと、いつ
ものように、おじいさんは丘に薪をとりに行きま
した。お弁当はおばあさんが作ってくれた大きな
おむすびです。お昼頃までせっせと働いたのでお
腹が空いてきました。働いたあとのおむすびは特
別においしいものです。おじいさんが地面に座り、
おむすびを取り出して食べようとしたとき、おむ
すびが手から落ち、丘を転がり始めました。

　「止まれ！　止まれ！　そのおむすびはばあさんが
作ってくれたんじゃ！」おじいさんは叫びながら追
いかけましたが、おむすびがどんどん転がり落ち
ていくので、捕まえることができません。ついに、
おむすびは丘の下の大きな穴に落ちてしまいまし
た。

Long, long ago, there lived an old man and his wife in a village. They were good and honest, and they worked hard, so people called them 'the good old couple.' One day, the old man went up the hill to get firewood as usual. He carried a big rice ball that his wife had made. After working hard all morning, he felt hungry. Eating a rice ball after work was one of his favorite things, so he sat on the ground and took one out. He was about to eat it when the rice ball fell out of his hands and landed on the ground. It started rolling down the hill.

"Stop! Stop! My wife made that rice ball!" shouted the old man. He started to run after it. But it kept rolling down so fast that he couldn't catch it. Finally, it fell into a big hole at the bottom of the hill.

「おやまあ！　ここにこんな大きな穴があったとはのう」おじいさんはそう言って穴をのぞき込むと、穴の中から歌が聞こえてきました。

「おむすびころりん。ころころりん」とてもきれいな歌だったので、もっとよく聞こえるようにと、おじいさんは穴の中に身を乗り出しました。すると、歌は止まりました。さらに奥へと首を突っ込むと、穴の中に落ちてしまいました。今度はこんな歌が聞こえてきました。「おじいさんころりん。ころころりん」

おじいさんは辺りを見回しました。穴の底から見上げると、そこは大きな広間のようでした。そこではねずみが大勢働いていました。白いねずみがやってきて言いました。「おじいさん、ぼくらの家にようこそ。大きなおむすびをありがとう。おばあさんが作ったの？　みんな大喜びです。お礼にお昼をごちそうします」

ねずみたちはみんな楽しそうに働いています。歌いながらおもちをついています。「ねこがいなければ、ここは平和。ねずみの世界は平和が好き。

"Oh, I never knew there was such a big hole here," he said. He looked down into the hole. He could hear a song coming from the hole.

"Rice ball rolling down. Rolling, rolling down." The song was so beautiful that he leaned into the hole so he could hear it better. The music stopped. He put his head deeper into the hole, and he fell down into it. This time the song he heard went, "Old man rolling down. Rolling, rolling down."

He looked around. He was at the bottom of the hole, but it looked like a big hall. There were a lot of mice working there. One of the white mice came up to him and said, "Welcome to our home, old man. Thank you so much for giving us that big rice ball. Did your wife make it? We're all really glad to have it. We'll give you lunch in return."

All the mice were working happily. They were making rice cakes and singing a song. They sang, "If there's no cat, our home will

ヨーホー。ヨーホーホー」

　ねずみはおじいさんにつきたてのおもちと食べ物をあげました。おじいさんは一口食べて言いました。「こんなにおいしいおもちは初めてじゃ」おじいさんはもらった食べ物を残さずたいらげました。一匹のねずみが小さいきれいな箱を持ってきて、おじいさんにあげました。「これはおばあさんへのおみやげです。おむすびがとてもおいしかった、ありがとうと伝えてください」

　その頃、おばあさんは、帰りの遅いおじいさんのことを心配していました。おじいさんが箱をかかえて帰ってくると、おばあさんはホッとして泣いてしまいました。おじいさんは帰りが遅くなった理由を話しました。持ってきた箱を開けると、中には小判と宝石が入っていました。その箱はねずみの宝箱だったのです。

　おじいさんとおばあさんはとても幸せでしたが、お話はまだ終わっていません。このやさしい二人の家の隣に、おじいさんとおばあさんがもう一組住んでいました。こちらの二人はやさしくもなく

be peaceful. We love peace in the world of mice. Yo-ho, yo-ho-ho."

The mice gave the man some fresh rice cakes and other food to eat. He took one bite and said, "This is the most delicious rice cake I've ever had in my life." He ate all the food they gave him. Then one of the mice brought a small, beautiful box. The mouse gave it to him and said, "This is for your wife. Would you tell her how much we liked her rice ball? This is to say thank you."

By that time, his wife had started worrying about her husband because he was late home. When he came back with the box, she cried with relief. The old man told her why he couldn't come home earlier and opened the box. There was money and jewelry in the box. It was a mouse treasure box.

The couple were very happy, but the story is not over. There lived another old couple next door to the good old couple's house. They were not nice and honest, and they

正直でもなく、働き者でもありませんでしたが、やさしいおじいさんとおばあさんの話を聞いて、ねずみの宝物がいっぱい入った箱がほしいと思いました。

　翌朝、よくばりなおじいさんは、おばあさんが作った大きなおむすびを持ってその丘に行きました。辺りを見回して、話に聞いていた穴を探しました。丘のてっぺんからふもとまで穴を探し回ると、穴は一番下のほうにありました。「きっとあれだ」と独り言を言い、おむすびを穴の中に落としました。まもなく穴から歌が聞こえてきました。

　「おむすびころりん。ころころりん」おじいさんは思わず笑いましたが、歌の最後の部分が聞こえてきません。もっとよく聞こえるようにと穴の中に身を乗り出すと、穴の中に落ちてしまいました。穴の底で辺りを見回すと、ねずみが大勢歌いながらおもちをついています。「きっとここだ」と独り言を言い、しばらく歌を聴いていました。ねずみたちは働きながらおじいさんをちらりと見ました。

didn't work hard either. They heard the good old couple's conversation and wanted to get a box full of mouse treasure.

The next morning, the bad old man went to the same hill with a big rice ball his wife had made. He looked around for the hole he had heard about. He searched the ground from the top of the hill to the bottom looking for the hole. He finally found it at the very bottom. "This must be the hole," he said to himself. He dropped his rice ball into the hole. Soon he heard a song coming out of the hole.

"Rice ball rolling down, rolling, rolling down." He laughed to himself, but he couldn't hear the last part of the song. He leaned into the hole to hear better, and fell into it. When he landed at the bottom, he looked around and saw a lot of mice singing and making rice cakes. "I'm sure this must be the place," he said to himself. He listened

みんな歌いながらおもちをついています。

　「ねこがいなければ、ここは平和。ねずみの世界
は平和が好き。ヨーホー。ヨーホーホー」

　よくばりなおじいさんはある考えを思いつきま
した。「ねこのまねをすれば、ねずみの宝物が手に
入るぞ」おじいさんはねこの鳴き声をまねて大きな
声で叫びました。
　突然、すべてのねずみの動きが止まりました。
次の瞬間、一匹のねずみが叫びました。「ねこだ！
ねこがいるぞ！」別のねずみが叫びました。「ねこ
を入れるな！　入口を閉じろ！」
　ねずみたちはみんな走り出しました。すぐに静
かになり、暗くなりました。
　おじいさんは暗闇に一人取り残され、どうした
らよいのかわかりませんでした。急に死ぬのが怖
くなってきて、ねずみの世界から逃げだそうと、
必死で手で土を掻き出し始めました。

　よくばりなおばあさんは杖なしでは歩けないほ

to the song for a while. The mice just looked at the old man as they worked. They were singing while they made rice cakes.

They sang, "If there's no cat, our place will be peaceful. We love peace in the world of mice. Yo-ho, yo-ho-ho."

The bad old man had an idea. He thought, "Maybe I can get the mouse treasure if I pretend to be a cat." He started to make loud cat noises.

Suddenly, all the mice stopped moving. The next moment one of them shouted, "A cat! There's a cat in here." Another mouse shouted, "Don't let him in. Close the entrance."

All the mice started running around. Soon it became quiet and dark.

The old man was left alone in the darkness and did not know what he should do. Suddenly, he became very afraid that he was going to die. He started to dig using just his hands to escape from the world of mice.

The bad old man's wife was too old to walk

ど年をとっていましたが、ねずみの宝物をわくわ
くして待っていました。家でじっと待っていられ
なくなり、手に杖を持ち、丘へと歩き出しました。
丘のふもとまで来ると疲れて歩けなくなったので、
おばあさんはしばらくそこで休むことにしました
が、ふと下を見ると、手前の地面が動いています。

「きっと畑を荒らすもぐらだ。憎たらしい。こら
しめてやろう」おばあさんはそう言って、杖で地面
を力いっぱいたたきました。

「やめてくれ！　お願いだ」おじいさんは叫びな
がら地面から飛び出しました。
　かわいそうなおばあさんはびっくり仰天して声
も出ません。さらに悪いことに、おじいさんは杖
で頭をたたかれ、大けがをしていました。二人と
もしばらく口もきけませんでした。

without a stick, but she was very excited about the mouse treasure. She could not wait at home, so with her stick in her hand, she started walking to the hill. When she reached the bottom of the hill, she was so tired that she couldn't walk anymore. She decided to stop there for a while and rest. She looked down and saw that the ground in front of her was moving.

"That must be the mole that damages our field. I hate it. I'll teach it a good lesson," she said. She began to beat the ground with her stick as hard as she could.

"Stop it, please!" shouted her husband as he jumped up from the ground.

The poor old woman was so surprised that she could not say anything. What was worse was that she had hurt the old man's head very badly with her stick. Neither of them could say anything for a while.

English Conversational Ability Test
国際英語会話能力検定

● E-CATとは…
英語が話せるようになるための
テストです。インターネット
ベースで、30分であなたの発
話力をチェックします。

www.ecatexam.com

● iTEP®とは…
世界各国の企業、政府機関、アメリカの大学
300校以上が、英語能力判定テストとして採用。
オンラインによる90分のテストで文法、リー
ディング、リスニング、ライティング、スピー
キングの5技能をスコア化。iTEP®は、留学、就
職、海外赴任などに必要な、世界に通用する英
語力を総合的に評価する画期的なテストです。

www.itepexamjapan.com

［対訳ニッポン双書］
日本昔ばなし【増補改訂版】
Long-ago Stories of Japan [Expanded Edition]

2011 年 6 月 8 日		初版	第 1 刷発行
2019 年 4 月 13 日			第 3 刷発行
2024 年 6 月 2 日	増補改訂版		第 1 刷発行
2024 年 9 月 6 日			第 2 刷発行

訳　者　　カルラ・ヴァレンタイン 他

発行者　　賀川　洋

発行所　　IBCパブリッシング株式会社
　　　　　〒162-0804 東京都新宿区中里町 29 番 3 号 菱秀神楽坂ビル
　　　　　Tel. 03-3513-4511 Fax. 03-3513-4512
　　　　　www.ibcpub.co.jp

印刷所　　株式会社シナノパブリッシングプレス

© IBC パブリッシング 2024
Printed in Japan

ISBN978-4-7946-0816-1